INSIDE THE COMFORT ZONE

TURN YOUR COMFORT ZONE INTO YOUR SECRET SUPER POWER

DR. ASHISH GUPTA

Made with ♥ on the Notion Press Platform
www.notionpress.com

To those who have been told that growth only happens outside their comfort zones, this book is for you.

Contents

Contents

Prologue

For as long as we can remember, we've been told that real growth lies on the other side of comfort. **"Step out of your comfort zone,"** they say, as though it's a badge of honor to abandon what we know and dive headfirst into the unknown. We're encouraged to stretch, to leap, to throw ourselves into discomfort because that's where life begins—or so we're told.

But what if there's a different path? What if **comfort isn't a limitation**, but a source of strength? What if staying in your comfort zone—owning it, mastering it, expanding it—could lead to an even greater kind of success?

This book invites you to rethink the concept of comfort. To scc it not as a placc of complacency, but as a powerful foundation for **excellence, confidence, and resilience**. Inside your comfort zone lies your **mastery zone**—the place where your skills, talents, and strengths converge, allowing you to operate at your best. Here, you can make thoughtful, deliberate decisions, develop your craft, and push boundaries without sacrificing stability. Here, you have a **vantage point** from which you can view opportunities with clarity, acting strategically rather than reactively.

This book is about **living powerfully within your comfort zone** and using it as a launchpad for growth, innovation, and influence. It's about redefining success to mean not a life of constant struggle and uncertainty but a journey marked by mastery, confidence, and fulfillment. It's about expanding your comfort zone on your own terms—stretching it, owning it, and allowing it to evolve as you do.

You won't find advice here to abandon what you know or to chase every unfamiliar challenge. Instead, you'll discover a path that honors what you've built, celebrates your strengths, and helps you expand in a sustainable, empowered way. Inside these pages, you'll learn how comfort can be the key to lasting success, a wellspring of resilience, and a powerful tool for achieving more by fully embracing who you are.

So, step into your comfort zone. Settle into it. Master it. Let's redefine what it means to grow, thrive, and succeed—starting from the ground up.

Welcome to ***Inside The Comfort Zone***.

About The Author

Ashish Gupta is a visionary thinker, author, and career strategist dedicated to challenging conventional wisdom and empowering individuals to achieve success on their own terms. With over 14 years of experience in higher education, career guidance, and personal development, Ashish has worked with some of India's top universities, helping students, professionals, and institutions navigate growth in an ever-evolving world.

With a deep-rooted passion for Indian wisdom and modern success strategies, Ashish has authored several books that blend traditional insights with contemporary career and personal development principles. Inside The Comfort Zone is his latest work, challenging the widely accepted notion that success only comes from stepping into discomfort.

Through his books, talks, and training programs, Ashish continues to inspire students, working professionals, entrepreneurs, and educators to harness their strengths, master their zones, and create sustainable, impactful success.

Introduction: The Comfort Zone Myth

CHAPTER ONE

Challenging Conventional Wisdom

For years, we've been fed the idea that "growth only happens outside your comfort zone." The mantra has become so pervasive that it feels like an undeniable truth. Motivational speakers, life coaches, and self-help gurus have tirelessly repeated this advice: "Get uncomfortable, take risks, and push beyond your limits." It's been portrayed as the only path to success, and any deviation from it is seen as stagnation.

But what if I told you that this widely accepted belief is, at best, only half true—and at worst, a damaging oversimplification?

The idea that success comes exclusively from leaving your comfort zone is one of those shallow mantras that sounds smart but lacks depth. It appeals to thrill-seekers, to those looking for immediate adrenaline rushes, but ignores the silent power of consistency, mastery, and deep focus that comes from staying in your comfort zone.

The Comfort Zone: A Space of Mastery, Not Complacency

The truth is, your comfort zone is not the enemy of growth. In fact, it's the exact opposite: your comfort zone is where you achieve mastery. It's the place where your skills, knowledge, and experiences converge to create a foundation of excellence. When you operate within your comfort zone, you are not being complacent—you are sharpening the tools you already possess to perfection.

This doesn't mean you shouldn't seek out new experiences or learn from challenges outside your comfort zone. Of course, you must explore, learn, and grow. But growth doesn't require abandoning what makes you strong. In fact, real success comes from expanding your comfort zone—taking what you know, fortifying it, and pushing its boundaries strategically.

Why Conventional Wisdom Fails

The common wisdom around "discomfort equals growth" fails because it ignores an important fact: not all discomfort is productive. Pushing yourself into unfamiliar territory can certainly result in growth, but it can just as easily lead to anxiety, burnout, or decision paralysis if done without purpose. Growth without direction is chaos. When you're constantly outside your comfort zone, you're too busy adapting to survive rather than improving to thrive.

When you recognize the value of your comfort zone as a space for growth and mastery, you are no longer at the mercy of the hustle culture. Instead, you become the architect of your own success, dictating when and where to push boundaries, and doing it on your own terms.

CHAPTER TWO

Why Staying Comfortable is Not Complacency

One of the biggest misconceptions in personal development is the idea that comfort equals complacency. We've been led to believe that if we're comfortable, we must not be growing. That if we're not constantly stepping into discomfort, we are settling for less.

But this notion is not only flawed; it can be destructive.

Comfort is the Foundation of Mastery

Staying in your comfort zone does not mean you've stopped improving. In fact, it is often where the most profound mastery occurs. When you operate within your comfort zone, you are in a state of peak performance. This is where you've accumulated expertise, sharpened your instincts, and gained precision in what you do.

Think about a surgeon performing a delicate procedure. Their comfort zone is the operating room, a space where they have honed their skills through repetition, practice, and experience. It's in this comfort zone that they save lives, not by taking unnecessary risks or trying untested methods, but by mastering their craft.

Success doesn't come from abandoning this zone of mastery; it comes from deepening it, perfecting it, and continuously improving upon what you already excel at. The true danger lies not in staying comfortable but in assuming that comfort prevents you from refining and advancing your expertise.

Complacency is Stagnation, Comfort is Stability

There is a critical difference between comfort and complacency. Complacency is a state of stagnation where there is no desire to grow, improve, or evolve. It is marked by laziness, lack of ambition, and a refusal to challenge oneself.

Comfort, on the other hand, is stability. It's a strong foundation from which you can grow strategically. When you stay in your comfort zone, you are not avoiding growth—you are ensuring that your growth is intentional, focused, and sustainable. It's the place where you gather your energy, practice your craft, and operate at your best.

Imagine a basketball player practicing free throws over and over again. The court is their comfort zone. Through repetition, they build muscle memory, improve precision, and become a reliable performer under pressure. Staying within this comfort zone doesn't make them complacent; it makes them exceptional at their skill.

Pushing Too Far Can Be Counterproductive

Many people think that stepping out of their comfort zone

automatically leads to success. But stepping too far too fast can often lead to burnout, anxiety, and even failure. When you leave your comfort zone for unfamiliar territory without preparation, you are entering a zone of uncertainty, where you may lack the skills, knowledge, or emotional readiness to succeed.

When you're constantly in a state of discomfort, you're not focused on mastering anything—you're focused on survival. And survival mode is not where growth happens. Growth happens when you have a solid foundation to build upon, and that foundation exists inside your comfort zone.

Strategic Growth From a Place of Strength

The real power comes from knowing when to stay in your comfort zone and when to stretch beyond it. Growth doesn't require you to constantly live in discomfort; it requires you to strategically push the boundaries of your comfort zone, little by little, so that it expands over time.

By mastering the space you already own, you create a strong, unshakable foundation. When you choose to step out of it, you do so with the strength and confidence gained from that mastery. You can explore new opportunities and challenges from a position of power, not fear.

In other words, staying comfortable allows you to grow smarter, not harder.

Your Comfort Zone - Your Most Secret Weapon

CHAPTER THREE

Redefining the Comfort Zone

We've all heard the phrase: "You need to get out of your comfort zone." It's thrown around in motivational talks, workplace meetings, and self-help books as if it were a universal truth. The comfort zone is often depicted as a place of stagnation, laziness, or missed opportunities. But what if we've been thinking about the comfort zone all wrong?

The Comfort Zone is Not a Prison, It's a Powerhouse

The traditional view of the comfort zone is that it's a bubble of inactivity, where nothing new happens and no growth occurs. This couldn't be further from the truth. The comfort zone, when redefined, is your foundation of competence. It's the space where you have developed your expertise, where you excel, and where you perform at your absolute best.

In fact, when you understand and master your comfort zone, you can use it as a launchpad to achieve more, not less. It is your personal domain where you thrive—where you control your environment, make the best decisions, and execute your skills with precision.

To think of the comfort zone as a limitation is to misunderstand its true power. It's not about confining yourself to a fixed space; it's about creating a stronghold, a place of mastery that you can expand.

The Zone of Mastery vs. The Zone of Stagnation

Let's be clear: staying comfortable doesn't mean you aren't pushing yourself to grow. It means you are leveraging your strengths, continuously improving what you already do well, and gradually expanding your expertise. This is the zone of mastery, where you focus on perfecting your craft.

On the other hand, the zone of stagnation is where complacency lives. This is where you stop caring about growth or improvement, where you refuse to push your boundaries or sharpen your skills. But the comfort zone and the stagnation zone are not the same. The former is where you build mastery, and the latter is where you fall into apathy. When you redefine the comfort zone as your powerhouse of excellence, it becomes clear that staying comfortable can be a catalyst for success—not a barrier.

The Myth of "Discomfort Equals Growth"

We've been conditioned to believe that discomfort automatically leads to growth. It's true that stepping into new challenges is an important part of personal and professional development. But discomfort, without direction or purpose, is just chaos. Not all discomfort is productive. In fact, discomfort can often lead to stress, burnout, and failure if approached recklessly.

Growth doesn't happen just because you're uncomfortable—it happens because you've strategically positioned yourself to grow. That's where the power of the comfort zone comes in. It's the place where you've built your strengths, and from this solid foundation, you can expand in a focused and deliberate way.

Stepping outside your comfort zone with no plan or preparation doesn't lead to growth. It leads to survival mode, where you're simply trying to get by rather than thrive. True growth happens when you push the boundaries of your comfort zone intelligently—moving into new challenges at your own pace, on your own terms, and equipped with the confidence that comes from mastering your current space.

Expanding, Not Escaping, Your Comfort Zone

Rather than trying to escape your comfort zone, the real goal should be to expand it. Think of your comfort zone as a muscle—it grows stronger with use and practice. When you push its boundaries, you're not abandoning it, you're expanding its reach.

The most successful people aren't those who constantly jump from one unfamiliar challenge to another. They are the ones who understand their strengths, work within them, and strategically step into new challenges that enhance those strengths. They use their comfort zone as a base of power, a place to recharge and refine their skills, then push its edges to include new areas of expertise.

Comfort as a Competitive Advantage

When you redefine your comfort zone, you realize that it's

not a liability—it's a competitive advantage. Your comfort zone is where you have the most control, the most clarity, and the most confidence. It's where you can dominate your space and make calculated moves toward growth.

Imagine a chess player who knows every move on the board but doesn't constantly chase chaos. Instead, they master the strategies they know best, refining and perfecting their approach. They don't abandon their comfort zone; they expand it, move by move, using their mastery to outthink their opponents. In the same way, your comfort zone is not something to leave behind—it's something to own, master, and leverage.

CHAPTER FOUR

Why It's the Base of Excellence

We often hear that stepping out of our comfort zone is essential for success. But what we don't hear enough is that staying in your comfort zone is what actually allows you to build excellence. Your comfort zone is not the enemy—it's the foundation from which you reach your highest potential.

Mastery Comes from Repetition

Excellence isn't achieved by constantly seeking out new, unfamiliar territory. It's achieved through consistent practice and refinement. Think of the world's top performers—elite athletes, master musicians, renowned surgeons. What do they have in common? They dedicate hours, years, and even decades to perfecting their craft within their comfort zone.

It's through repetition that they build muscle memory, hone their skills, and achieve a level of precision that sets them apart. Repetition allows you to refine your abilities, understand the nuances of your craft, and operate with a level of expertise that only comes from staying within your comfort zone long enough to master it.

Your comfort zone is where you perfect your craft. It's where you get to test your skills in a controlled environment, push your limits strategically, and focus on continuous improvement without the distractions of uncertainty.

Focus, Precision, and Clarity

In your comfort zone, you have the clarity of mind to focus deeply on what you do best. When you operate in a space you've mastered, distractions are minimized, and your mental energy isn't drained by stress or fear of the unknown. This clarity allows you to make faster, better decisions and operate with a higher level of precision.

Excellence requires focus. It's hard to achieve that focus when you're constantly stepping into unfamiliar, uncomfortable situations. When you're operating outside of your comfort zone, much of your energy is spent simply trying to adapt and survive. But inside your comfort zone, you have the mental bandwidth to aim for higher levels of performance. It's here that you can analyze your mistakes, tweak your strategies, and achieve a deeper understanding of your craft.

The Zone of Flow

The concept of flow—a state where you're fully immersed and performing at your best—often happens in your comfort zone. Flow is that optimal state of focus where time seems to disappear, and everything you do feels almost effortless. It's in this state that true excellence is born.

Flow doesn't happen in a constant state of discomfort. It happens when you are challenged just enough to push your boundaries but still feel in control. This is the sweet spot where your comfort zone begins to stretch, but not break. It's a state where your skills are matched with the task at hand, allowing you to push toward mastery without feeling overwhelmed.

By staying in your comfort zone long enough to reach flow, you create an environment where you can achieve peak performance regularly.

Confidence Fuels Excellence

Confidence is the bedrock of high performance. And where does confidence come from? It comes from knowing your abilities, trusting your instincts, and having control over your environment—all of which happen within your comfort zone.

When you operate in a space you've mastered, you build a reservoir of confidence. You know you've done the work, you've put in the hours, and you've refined your approach. This confidence allows you to take calculated risks and stretch yourself in new directions without feeling like you're losing control. The more confident you become, the more willing you are to push the edges of your comfort zone to expand it further, fueling a cycle of continuous growth.

Without the foundation of confidence built in your comfort zone, stepping into new challenges would feel overwhelming and chaotic. But when you've mastered your space, you can approach new opportunities from a position of strength, rather than fear.

Excellence Requires Stability

While the world glorifies the idea of constantly being uncomfortable, the truth is that excellence requires a certain level of stability. You need a strong foundation to build something great. Just as a house cannot stand without a solid base, you cannot achieve excellence without a firm grounding in your comfort zone.

Stability in your comfort zone doesn't mean you're not growing—it means you're setting yourself up for sustainable, long-term success. From this stable base, you can take measured steps into new challenges without destabilizing yourself. It allows you to control the pace of your growth, making sure that you're improving strategically, not recklessly.

The Competitive Advantage of Mastery

When you've mastered your comfort zone, you gain a competitive advantage. Most people are so eager to jump into the next challenge that they never fully master the space they're in. But mastery gives you an edge—an ability to perform at a level that others simply cannot match. It's where you dominate your field, where your expertise becomes second nature, and where you can outperform your competition with precision.

Excellence isn't about being constantly uncomfortable. It's about mastering your strengths, leveraging them strategically, and expanding them when you're ready. When you view your comfort zone as the base of excellence, you unlock its true potential.

The Secret Power of Mastery

CHAPTER FIVE

Mastery Through Repetition

In a world obsessed with new challenges and constant change, we often overlook one of the most powerful principles of excellence: **repetition.** True mastery, whether in sports, art, business, or any other field, comes not from dabbling in a variety of pursuits, but from honing a skill over and over until it becomes second nature. This is where the comfort zone reveals its true power.

The Power of Repetition

Repetition is not the enemy of growth; it is the engine of mastery. It allows you to go beyond surface-level understanding and dig deeper into the nuances of your craft. Repetition turns knowledge into instinct. It transforms a basic skill into an art form. By repeating actions in a controlled, familiar environment—your comfort zone—you are able to refine your performance to the point of near-perfection.

Consider athletes, musicians, and craftspeople. They don't achieve greatness by constantly trying new techniques or pushing themselves into uncomfortable territories. Instead, they reach the pinnacle of their fields by practicing the same moves, strokes, or notes over and over again. This repetition builds muscle memory and precision, enabling them to perform at an elite level when it matters most.

Practice Makes Permanent

The old saying, "practice makes perfect," is misleading. In reality, practice makes permanent. The more you repeat an action, the more it becomes ingrained in your mind and body. Whether it's hitting a tennis ball, giving a presentation, or solving a complex problem, repetition allows you to embed the skills into your subconscious. Eventually, what once required conscious effort becomes automatic.

This is the essence of mastery. You no longer have to think about the individual steps; your mind and body work in unison to execute flawlessly. When you're operating from this state of flow, your comfort zone becomes the place where true excellence is achieved. You are not just performing well—you are performing effortlessly.

The Danger of Constantly Seeking Newness

In the pursuit of growth, many people fall into the trap of constantly seeking out new challenges or unfamiliar tasks. While novelty can stimulate learning, it can also distract you from achieving depth in any one area. Moving from one challenge to the next without mastering the basics leads to scattered progress rather than true expertise.

Repetition, on the other hand, gives you the focus needed to refine your skills and make lasting improvements. Each time you repeat an action, you gain new insights, uncover subtle details, and push your limits incrementally. Mastery is built on this foundation of steady, consistent progress, not on the rush to always try something new.

From Repetition to Innovation

Some of the most groundbreaking innovations come from people who have mastered repetition. Once you have mastered the basics and developed expertise in your comfort zone, you can start to innovate. Innovation doesn't come from abandoning what you know—it comes from building on it. When you've practiced something to the point of mastery, you can start experimenting with new techniques or approaches within that field, because you understand the rules well enough to bend or break them.

Think of a chef who has mastered classic cooking techniques. Only after years of perfecting traditional dishes can they confidently experiment with new flavors, textures, or presentations. Their mastery of repetition allows them to push the boundaries, not by abandoning their comfort zone, but by expanding it in new, exciting ways.

Consistency Over Intensity

Another benefit of repetition is that it fosters consistency. Mastery is not achieved through occasional bursts of effort but through sustained, disciplined practice over time. Many people make the mistake of focusing on intensity—believing that short periods of extreme effort will lead to success. But true excellence comes from the cumulative effect of consistent effort.

This is why staying in your comfort zone—where you can practice with consistency and focus—leads to long-term mastery. Each time you repeat a task, you refine your process, sharpen your skills, and improve incrementally. Over time, this leads to exponential growth, far surpassing the results of short, intense efforts outside your comfort zone.

The Comfort Zone as a Place for Mastery

The comfort zone is often misunderstood as a place where growth stagnates. In reality, it's where mastery is built. Repetition requires a certain level of stability—an environment where you can focus without distraction, where you can make mistakes and learn from them, and where you can perfect your skills at your own pace. This stability exists inside your comfort zone, making it the ideal space for long-term growth.

When you view your comfort zone as a place of mastery rather than stagnation, you unlock its full potential. You begin to see repetition not as something boring or redundant, but as a tool to achieve excellence. Each repetition brings you closer to perfection, turning your comfort zone into a powerhouse of skill, precision, and expertise.

CHAPTER SIX

How Comfort Zones Build Precision and Clarity

When people think about growth, they often focus on big, bold moves that push boundaries and break limits. While stepping outside your comfort zone can lead to new experiences, staying within your comfort zone can lead to something even more valuable—precision and clarity. Mastery isn't just about doing more; it's about doing better. And the comfort zone provides the perfect environment for achieving that.

The Power of Focus

Your comfort zone is the place where you are most at ease, but it's also where you're most focused. You're not distracted by the unknown or overwhelmed by unfamiliar challenges. Instead, you're working in a space where your skills are sharp, your mind is clear, and your energy is directed toward refining what you already know.

When you're in this zone of comfort, you can focus on the small details that often get overlooked when you're trying to juggle too many new things at once. This focus allows you to operate with precision. You're not just performing tasks—you're performing them with a level of expertise that only comes from deep understanding and repetitive practice.

Eliminating Noise and Distraction

Outside the comfort zone, you're often in a state of survival—adapting to new circumstances, learning on the fly, and managing uncertainty. This constant pressure creates a lot of noise and distraction, pulling your attention in multiple directions at once. As a result, you may be less effective, operating more on instinct and reaction than on thoughtful action.

Inside your comfort zone, however, that noise is minimized. You're not fighting the distractions of the unfamiliar, so you have the mental space to work on refining your approach. This clarity helps you see your tasks more clearly, giving you the chance to notice subtle details and perfect your performance. When you eliminate distractions, you are free to fine-tune your actions with laser-like focus.

Perfecting the Craft Through Consistency

Precision isn't something that happens by chance—it's developed through consistent effort. When you operate within your comfort zone, you can repeat tasks with the goal of constant improvement. Over time, each small refinement adds up, leading to significant gains in both accuracy and efficiency.

Consistency is the key to building clarity in what you do. Whether you're perfecting a skill, running a business, or managing a team, the consistent application of your strengths leads to clearer, more predictable results. This repetition provides a clear roadmap for improvement, helping you eliminate guesswork and hone in on what works best.

The Comfort Zone as a Safe Space for Reflection

One of the greatest advantages of the comfort zone is that it provides a space for reflection. Without the immediate pressure to adapt to new or uncomfortable situations, you have the opportunity to reflect on your actions, identify what's working, and improve on what isn't.

Reflection is crucial for clarity. It allows you to take a step back, analyze your performance, and understand the nuances of your work. When you operate outside of your comfort zone, the rush of new challenges often prevents you from reflecting in the moment. However, in your comfort zone, you have the time and mental space to think deeply, analyze results, and adjust your approach to achieve better outcomes.

Building Precision Through Small Adjustments

In your comfort zone, you can make incremental adjustments to your actions. Instead of making broad, sweeping changes, you can focus on refining the small details that make a big difference. These small adjustments compound over time, leading to greater precision and effectiveness in your work.

Whether you're working on your communication skills, developing a product, or honing a technical skill, the ability to make these small, steady improvements is what leads to mastery. The comfort zone gives you the stability and consistency to make these adjustments without the stress of major changes or risky leaps.

Clarity Comes from Control

Clarity is about having a clear understanding of your strengths, your goals, and the actions that lead to success. In your comfort zone, you have control over your environment, your actions, and your outcomes. This control fosters a sense of confidence and competence that is crucial for achieving clarity.

When you're in control, you can make decisions more effectively. You know your capabilities, you understand the situation, and you can focus on executing your plans with confidence. This clarity in decision-making allows you to avoid unnecessary risks and focus on areas where you can have the most impact.

Operating outside of your comfort zone often means you're reacting to external pressures and navigating uncertainty. This can cloud your judgment and make it harder to achieve clarity. But inside your comfort zone, you're able to control the narrative, set the pace, and focus on what truly matters.

Precision as a Competitive Edge

In any field, those who operate with precision tend to rise above the rest. Precision allows you to perform tasks with greater accuracy, efficiency, and confidence. It's what sets the master apart from the beginner—the ability to do things right, time and time again, with minimal error.

Your comfort zone, when leveraged properly, becomes the place where you sharpen your precision. Whether you're refining a specific skill or developing a broader strategy, operating within a zone you've mastered allows you to work at a level of detail that others may overlook. This precision gives you a competitive edge, enabling you to deliver results that are consistently high-quality.

Don't Abandon Your Comfort Zone

CHAPTER SEVEN

Why Leaving Your Comfort Zone Isn't Always Necessary

We live in a world that constantly glorifies hustle, risk-taking, and bold leaps into the unknown, there is an underlying assumption: if you're not uncomfortable, you're not growing. While there's some truth to the idea that new experiences and challenges can lead to growth, the belief that you must always leave your comfort zone to succeed is a misleading oversimplification.

In fact, leaving your comfort zone isn't always necessary. There are many situations where staying within it—or strategically expanding it—leads to even greater success. The comfort zone, when mastered, can be your greatest asset.

Mastery Comes From Staying Inside

Leaving your comfort zone might provide new experiences, but staying inside your comfort zone allows you to achieve mastery. Growth isn't only about doing new things; it's also about doing familiar things exceptionally well.

Think about top professionals in any field—whether it's a musician mastering their instrument, an athlete perfecting their performance, or a business leader honing their strategy. They don't achieve greatness by constantly seeking out discomfort. Instead, they spend countless hours refining their skills, gaining deep expertise, and working within their zone of mastery. This repeated focus within their comfort zone enables them to deliver outstanding results.

Strategic Growth Without Chaos

The assumption that growth requires discomfort often leads to chaos. When you push too far beyond what you know, you risk entering unfamiliar territory without the necessary tools, skills, or confidence to succeed. In this situation, you're not growing—you're just surviving. The energy that could be used for mastery is instead spent on scrambling to adapt and avoid failure.

Strategic growth, on the other hand, happens when you push the boundaries of your comfort zone in a controlled way. Instead of jumping into the unknown, you gradually expand your area of expertise. By stepping just beyond your current limits, but still within your zone of mastery, you ensure that you're not overwhelmed. This gradual expansion allows for growth that is sustainable, effective, and—most importantly—on your terms.

Consistency Over Disruption

One of the biggest advantages of staying within your comfort zone is the ability to maintain consistency. Growth doesn't always come from extreme change. More often than not, it's the result of small, consistent improvements over time.

Leaving your comfort zone may bring short-term excitement, but it can also disrupt the consistency needed for long-term mastery. Whether it's building a new habit, learning a skill, or working toward a goal, consistency is key. In your comfort zone, you have the mental clarity, control, and focus to perform at your best, day in and day out.

It's this consistency—born from stability—that leads to mastery. By staying within your comfort zone, you allow yourself the time and space to repeat tasks, refine your approach, and make small adjustments that lead to significant improvement over time.

Panic Mode vs. Peak Performance

When people force themselves out of their comfort zones too aggressively, they often find themselves in panic mode. This state is not conducive to growth. In panic mode, you're more focused on surviving than thriving. Your mind is filled with uncertainty, stress, and anxiety, making it difficult to perform at your best.

In contrast, peak performance happens in a space where you are comfortable—where you know the terrain, understand the rules, and can focus on refining your actions. This is where the comfort zone shines. It's not about stagnation; it's about creating an environment where you can perform at your highest level because you're operating from a place of confidence and control.

The Comfort Zone as a Launchpad

Leaving your comfort zone isn't always necessary because your comfort zone itself can be a powerful launchpad for growth. When you have mastered the basics and gained expertise in your domain, you can use that mastery as a base to strategically explore new challenges.

This doesn't mean staying in your comfort zone forever. It means recognizing that your comfort zone is a space for preparation, practice, and precision. When you're ready to step into new challenges, you're doing so from a position of strength, not weakness. You're not blindly jumping into the unknown—you're bringing the skills, knowledge, and confidence you've developed in your comfort zone with you.

Leveraging Your Strengths for Success

One of the biggest misconceptions about comfort zones is that they are places where you become stagnant. But in reality, your comfort zone is where your strengths lie. It's where you perform your best, where your skills are sharpest, and where you are most confident. Leaving it behind doesn't always make sense.

Instead of abandoning your strengths, leverage them. Use your comfort zone as a base of power, where you can build upon what you already do well. In many cases, success comes not from constantly seeking discomfort, but from doubling down on your strengths and expanding from there.

Great leaders, athletes, and professionals don't succeed by abandoning their strengths. They thrive by mastering their game, refining their skills, and strategically pushing the boundaries of their comfort zone to explore new opportunities—without leaving the mastery they've built behind.

Growth Without Burnout

Leaving your comfort zone can lead to burnout if done recklessly. Constantly pushing yourself into discomfort—without a solid foundation—can drain your energy and enthusiasm. It creates stress and can cause you to lose focus on what truly matters.

In contrast, staying in your comfort zone allows for sustainable growth. It's where you can pace yourself, avoid unnecessary stress, and create an environment for long-term success. By growing within your comfort zone, you avoid the crash-and-burn cycle that often comes from chasing discomfort for the sake of it.

Expanding, Not Escaping

The key isn't to leave your comfort zone; it's to expand it. By strategically pushing the boundaries of what you're comfortable with, you can grow without losing the benefits of the mastery you've already developed. Each time you expand your comfort zone, it becomes larger, encompassing more skills, experiences, and opportunities.

This approach ensures that your growth is steady and purposeful. Instead of jumping into the unknown without preparation, you're building on a solid foundation, ensuring that each step forward is supported by the strength of what you've already mastered.

CHAPTER EIGHT

Success Stories of Mastering the Known

While society often celebrates those who step into the unknown, many of the world's most successful individuals have achieved greatness by mastering what they already know. Their success didn't come from constantly seeking out discomfort but from refining and perfecting their craft within their comfort zone. These stories highlight the power of repetition, focus, and deep expertise.

1. Late Sir Ratan Tata: Redefining Indian Industry Through Mastery and Vision

Late Sir Ratan Tata, the esteemed chairman emeritus of the Tata Group, is a perfect example of how mastering the known can bring transformative change. Born into the Tata family, Ratan Tata grew up surrounded by the legacy of Indian industry. However, instead of stepping away to explore unrelated fields, he committed himself to building upon the Tata Group's legacy—mastering the art of business, leadership, and strategy.

Ratan Tata's approach was both innovative and deeply grounded in what he knew. He used his understanding of the Tata Group's strengths to lead it into new territories while retaining its core values of trust and integrity. The acquisition of Jaguar Land Rover and the launch of the Tata Nano are just two examples of his ability to expand Tata's influence without abandoning its foundation. His story shows that staying grounded in your comfort zone—your area of mastery—can lead to remarkable achievements when combined with vision and persistence.

2. A.R. Rahman: Mastering Music, Transforming the Sound of a Nation

A.R. Rahman, the "Mozart of Madras," began his career in a domain he knew intimately—music. With a foundation in Indian classical music and early exposure to sound engineering, Rahman spent years mastering his craft. He didn't feel the need to abandon his roots or seek out unfamiliar genres. Instead, he expanded his comfort zone within the music industry, blending his classical training with modern production techniques to create a unique sound that resonated globally.

Rahman's dedication to his art within the familiar realm of Indian music allowed him to elevate it to an international platform. His success—from winning Oscars for Slumdog Millionaire to collaborating with global artists—shows that mastering what you know can lead to global innovation. Rahman's journey illustrates that true mastery allows you to push boundaries from within, transforming and elevating your craft while staying connected to your roots.

3. Amitabh Bachchan: Reinventing Himself Within the Familiar World of Cinema

Amitabh Bachchan is not only one of India's most celebrated actors but also a testament to the power of reinvention within one's comfort zone. Starting with roles in the 1970s as the "angry young man," Bachchan became a household name in India. Instead of diversifying into unrelated fields, he deepened his mastery in acting, exploring different genres, characters, and narratives that allowed him to stay relevant and powerful in a rapidly evolving industry.

When Bachchan faced financial setbacks in the late 1990s, he didn't leave the world of cinema. Instead, he pivoted within it, mastering television with Kaun Banega Crorepati and rebuilding his brand through film roles that showcased his versatility and wisdom. His career demonstrates that you don't need to leave your comfort zone to grow—sometimes the best growth happens when you stay within your field and find ways to adapt, improve, and reinvent yourself.

4. Sundar Pichai: Mastering Technology, Scaling Up Influence Globally

Sundar Pichai, CEO of Alphabet Inc. and Google, started his journey by mastering the domain he knew best: technology and product innovation. Hailing from Tamil Nadu and educated in engineering and material sciences, Pichai entered Google and focused on product management—a space where he could fully leverage his technical skills. Rather than seeking out diverse roles, he dedicated himself to becoming a master of product development, working on Chrome, Android, and other flagship products that define Google today.

Pichai's journey shows that success doesn't require constant reinvention; it can also come from building depth within your area of expertise. His ascent to Google's leadership shows how mastery in a specific domain can not only bring personal success but also drive impactful change within an entire industry. By embracing and perfecting the known, Pichai demonstrated that growth can be a natural progression of deepening and expanding expertise.

5. Dr. Devi Shetty: Transforming Healthcare Through Expertise and Mastery

Dr. Devi Shetty, a pioneering cardiac surgeon and founder of Narayana Health, exemplifies how mastering the known can revolutionize an industry. From a young age, Shetty focused on healthcare, dedicating his life to mastering the field of heart surgery. He didn't step away from medicine to explore unrelated challenges; instead, he found ways to expand his impact from within, using his medical expertise to develop an affordable healthcare model that has transformed access to heart surgery in India.

Dr. Shetty's ability to leverage his mastery in surgery allowed him to create a healthcare network that has served thousands of patients who otherwise couldn't afford it. His journey shows that living powerfully within your mastery zone doesn't mean limiting your impact—it means finding innovative ways to make a difference within your field. By staying true to his medical roots, Dr. Shetty achieved remarkable growth that benefited not only his career but society at large.

6. Narayana Murthy: Mastering the Business of IT to Put India on the Global Map

Narayana Murthy, the co-founder of Infosys, is another inspiring example of mastering the known for success. In the 1980s, Murthy could have ventured into diverse industries, but he chose to focus on the emerging field of information technology. With a deep understanding of technology and a commitment to excellence, he focused on building Infosys from the ground up, using his knowledge of IT to bring Indian expertise to the global stage.

Murthy's commitment to mastering the known field of technology positioned Infosys as a pioneer in Indian IT and a global player. By staying true to his expertise, Murthy demonstrated that mastering the known can not only lead to personal success but also put an entire industry on the map. His story shows how dedication to one's field can lead to innovations that drive national progress.

7. Michael Jordan – Mastering the Fundamentals of Basketball

Michael Jordan is considered one of the greatest basketball players of all time, and his success wasn't the result of constantly pushing into new, uncharted territory. Instead, Jordan's legendary performance on the court came from an obsessive focus on the fundamentals of the game—mastering his comfort zone.

Jordan famously spent hours practicing basic drills like shooting, dribbling, and footwork. By repeating these drills daily, he honed his skills to an unparalleled level of precision. His focus on perfecting the fundamentals enabled him to perform at his best, even under pressure. Jordan didn't achieve greatness by constantly seeking new challenges outside of basketball. Instead, he dominated his game by mastering what he already knew, pushing the limits of his comfort zone, and elevating his skills to legendary status.

8. Steve Jobs – Mastering Simplicity in Innovation

Steve Jobs, co-founder of Apple, revolutionized the tech world not by constantly chasing after new trends, but by mastering the art of simplicity within his comfort zone of product design. Jobs was known for his obsession with creating products that were intuitive, simple, and elegant—focusing on perfecting the known rather than constantly seeking out new and complex ideas.

Apple's success was built on the idea of refining products that people already used, such as computers, phones, and music players, rather than creating entirely new categories of technology. Jobs focused on mastering the user experience, simplifying it, and making it accessible to everyone. His comfort zone was understanding what people needed and delivering it with excellence. This mastery of the known led Apple to become one of the most successful companies in the world.

9. Warren Buffett – The Power of Staying Within Your Circle of Competence

Warren Buffett, one of the most successful investors of all time, is a perfect example of someone who has built his career by staying within his comfort zone—what he calls his "circle of competence." Buffett's investment strategy is grounded in his deep understanding of specific industries and businesses. Rather than chasing trends or venturing into areas where he lacks expertise, Buffett sticks to what he knows best: companies with strong fundamentals.

Buffett famously avoids investing in sectors or technologies he doesn't understand. By staying in his comfort zone, he has been able to focus on making smart, calculated decisions that have resulted in immense financial success. His approach shows that you don't need to constantly step into new areas to grow; sometimes, staying within what you know and perfecting it is the key to long-term success.

10. J.K. Rowling – Mastering the World of Harry Potter

J.K. Rowling didn't achieve success by constantly moving into new genres or types of writing. Instead, she became one of the world's most famous authors by mastering a single universe: the world of Harry Potter. Rowling spent years developing and refining her knowledge of this fictional world, perfecting the characters, storylines, and themes that made her books so beloved.

Rather than jumping from one type of writing to another, Rowling stayed in her comfort zone, creating a rich and deeply detailed universe that captivated millions of readers. Her focus on mastering one story world, rather than constantly seeking out new challenges, allowed her to create a global phenomenon that continues to resonate with readers of all ages.

Mastering the Known as a Path to Success

The success stories show that mastery of the known—rather than constantly venturing into the unknown—can lead to greatness. These individuals achieved extraordinary success not by chasing discomfort but by perfecting their skills and knowledge within their comfort zones.

Their stories illustrate that staying in your comfort zone and mastering what you know can be a powerful path to success. Mastery, repetition, and focus are often more effective than constantly seeking out new challenges. These individuals didn't need to abandon their comfort zones to grow—they expanded and refined them to achieve excellence.

Comfort Zone vs. Fear Zone

CHAPTER NINE

Understanding the Difference Between Comfort and Complacency

One of the most misunderstood aspects of personal growth is the confusion between comfort and complacency. They are often used interchangeably, but they represent two very different mindsets. Comfort is a space of confidence, mastery, and stability; complacency is a state of stagnation, laziness, and lack of ambition. Understanding the distinction between these two can be the key to unlocking sustainable growth and long-term success.

Comfort: The Zone of Mastery

Comfort is often portrayed negatively in today's hustle-driven world, where the focus is on constantly seeking discomfort and new challenges. But in reality, comfort is a place of strength. It's where you know the terrain, you've mastered your craft, and you can perform at your highest level. In this space, you can hone your skills, deepen your knowledge, and operate with precision.

Comfort allows you to maintain focus and clarity, free from the anxiety of navigating unfamiliar situations. This doesn't mean you're not growing—it means you're growing from a solid foundation. Comfort is the space where you are in control, which allows you to take measured risks, push boundaries at your own pace, and make strategic decisions from a position of strength. It's where you can thrive, not just survive.

Complacency: The Zone of Stagnation

Complacency, on the other hand, is where growth truly stalls. It's not about being comfortable; it's about being content with mediocrity. Complacency happens when you stop challenging yourself, when you settle for "good enough" instead of striving for excellence. It's marked by a lack of curiosity, ambition, and effort. While comfort is a foundation for growth, complacency is a barrier to it.

Complacency is dangerous because it often goes unnoticed. It can creep in when you've achieved a certain level of success or when you're no longer striving to improve. It's a mindset that says, "I've done enough," and it's this mindset that leads to stagnation. Unlike comfort, complacency doesn't provide room for refining skills or exploring new opportunities—it leads to a plateau where progress halts.

The Productive Zone of Comfort vs. The Passive State of Complacency

The key difference between comfort and complacency lies

in how you approach them. Comfort is productive. It's where you can practice, refine, and master what you do best. In this zone, you're focused, deliberate, and committed to getting better—even if the changes are incremental.

In contrast, complacency is passive. It's where you stop pushing forward, where the desire for improvement fades, and where you become satisfied with the status quo. You might still be performing tasks, but there's no intention behind your actions, no drive to excel. It's the difference between actively improving and merely coasting.

Growth in Comfort: Why Staying Comfortable Doesn't Mean Staying Stagnant

The common wisdom that says you must leave your comfort zone to grow is only partially true. While new experiences are essential for learning, growth doesn't always require abandoning your comfort zone. In fact, the comfort zone is often the best place to grow—strategically.

When you're in your comfort zone, you have the clarity and focus to make incremental improvements, perfect your craft, and master your skills. This is a productive kind of growth—one that builds on what you already know and pushes you to become better in areas where you already excel. Growth in this zone doesn't mean staying stagnant; it means refining and enhancing what you're already good at. It's about optimizing and expanding, not merely coasting.

Signs of Comfort vs. Signs of Complacency

Understanding whether you're in a state of comfort or complacency requires some self-awareness. Here are some signs to differentiate between the two:

Comfort:

- You feel confident and in control of your environment.
- You're refining your skills and improving steadily, even if the progress is incremental.
- You're excited about deepening your expertise in a specific area.
- You're continuously setting and meeting goals within your zone of mastery.
- You feel a sense of satisfaction from your work, but you still see room for growth.

Complacency:

- You feel uninterested in learning or trying anything new.
- You're satisfied with where you are, even if you're not performing at your best.
- You avoid setting new goals because you feel like you've "made it."
- You lack the motivation to improve or explore new opportunities.
- You feel stuck or disengaged from your work but don't take action to change it.
- Breaking Free from Complacency While Staying Comfortable

It's entirely possible to push boundaries and grow while staying in your comfort zone. The goal is to avoid slipping into complacency.

Here's how you can do that:

Set New Challenges Within Your Zone of Mastery: Even if you're staying within your comfort zone, you can still set new goals and challenges. Whether it's refining a skill, learning more about your field, or improving your processes, aim for constant improvement.

Seek Feedback Regularly: Sometimes we become complacent without realizing it. Regular feedback from mentors, colleagues, or clients can help you see where you might be stagnating. It's also a great way to identify areas for growth that you may not have considered.

Keep a Growth Mindset: Comfort doesn't mean you should stop learning. Stay curious, read, and continue developing your knowledge, even if you're already an expert. A growth mindset ensures that you remain engaged and focused on improvement.

Expand Your Comfort Zone Strategically: Instead of leaping into unknown and uncomfortable territory, push the boundaries of your comfort zone gradually. This allows you to grow without losing the confidence and clarity that comes from being in a space you know well.

Track Your Progress: Complacency often sneaks in when we lose track of our progress. By regularly evaluating your performance and setting milestones, you can stay engaged and motivated. It reminds you that you're on a path of growth, even within your comfort zone.

The Key to Sustained Growth

The confusion between comfort and complacency can lead people to believe that comfort is the enemy of growth. But the reality is quite different. Comfort provides the foundation for excellence, giving you the stability, confidence, and focus to master your craft. Complacency, however, is what happens when you stop pushing yourself—when you settle for less than you're capable of achieving.

By understanding the difference between these two states, you can stay in your comfort zone without falling into complacency. This allows for continuous growth, mastery, and success—on your own terms.

CHAPTER TEN

The Dangers of Entering the Fear Zone

We've all heard the advice: "Step out of your comfort zone." While this mantra encourages personal growth, there's an important aspect often left unspoken—**the fear zone that lies beyond your comfort zone**. This is the zone where anxiety, self-doubt, and insecurity thrive, and where the pursuit of growth can easily turn into survival mode. The fear zone, when entered recklessly or without preparation, can hinder progress rather than foster it.

What is the Fear Zone?

The fear zone is what you encounter when you push too far beyond your comfort zone, too fast, without the necessary tools, preparation, or mindset. It's a space marked by uncertainty, lack of control, and overwhelming doubt. Instead of healthy challenges that encourage growth, the fear zone often triggers stress, anxiety, and even paralysis.

While discomfort can sometimes lead to personal development, the fear zone is where discomfort turns into chaos. Here, you're not pushing boundaries productively; you're simply trying to survive and make sense of an environment that feels unpredictable and unmanageable.

Fear vs. Productive Discomfort

There's a difference between stepping into a zone of productive discomfort, where you can push boundaries and explore new opportunities, and entering a zone where fear dominates. In productive discomfort, you're still in control. You might face new challenges, but they're within a range you can handle. These challenges are designed to stretch your abilities without overwhelming you.

In the fear zone, however, you lose that control. The new challenges become so unfamiliar and intense that they evoke fear rather than curiosity. Instead of using discomfort as a tool for growth, fear becomes a barrier that stops you from making rational decisions and taking measured risks.

The Paralysis of Uncertainty

One of the greatest dangers of the fear zone is the paralysis of uncertainty. When you step too far outside your comfort zone, you may find yourself overwhelmed by the unknown. This paralysis can manifest in different ways: you might freeze and avoid taking action, or you might make impulsive decisions in an attempt to regain control.

Fear clouds your judgment. In the fear zone, your focus shifts from growth to survival, and your ability to think critically and strategically is compromised. Instead of improving or expanding your skills, you become preoccupied with navigating the unfamiliar, making it difficult to achieve any real progress.

Fear Breeds Self-Doubt

When you enter the fear zone, your inner critic often takes over. Self-doubt creeps in, making you question your abilities, your choices, and even your worth. This kind of internal dialogue can be incredibly damaging, as it erodes your confidence and motivation.

In this space, you're more likely to make decisions based on fear rather than logic or strategy. You may avoid risks altogether, not because they aren't worth taking, but because fear convinces you that failure is inevitable. Over time, this self-doubt can become ingrained, leading to a pattern of inaction and a mindset that limits your potential.

The Exhaustion of Constant Fear

Operating in the fear zone isn't sustainable. While brief moments of fear can be motivating, prolonged exposure to it leads to burnout. When you're constantly in a state of fight-or-flight, your mental, emotional, and physical resources are drained. Fear triggers stress responses that, over time, take a toll on your energy levels, decision-making ability, and overall well-being.

Living in a state of constant fear—whether it's fear of failure, fear of judgment, or fear of the unknown—prevents you from accessing the calm and clarity needed for thoughtful growth. Instead of working toward your goals, you're just trying to cope with the anxiety and stress. This can lead to exhaustion and, eventually, disengagement from the very challenges you set out to conquer.

Fear Zone as a Barrier to Mastery

Mastery doesn't come from being in a constant state of fear. It comes from a place of calm, focus, and deliberate practice. In the fear zone, however, your focus shifts from improvement to survival. You're too busy trying to manage the uncertainty and stress to dedicate time to refining your skills or learning new ones.

When you spend too much time in the fear zone, you risk stalling your progress entirely. Instead of moving forward, you're stuck in a loop of anxiety and second-guessing. Mastery requires stability, repetition, and clarity—all of which are hard to achieve when you're operating from a place of fear.

Knowing When to Pull Back

One of the most important skills in personal development is knowing when to pull back from the fear zone. Recognizing that you've pushed too far doesn't mean you've failed; it means you're being strategic. It's important to listen to your instincts when fear overwhelms you and step back to reassess the situation.

When you feel yourself slipping into the fear zone, pause and ask yourself:

- Am I losing focus on my goals?
- Is fear driving my decisions?
- Am I feeling paralyzed or stuck?
- Do I need more preparation or support before tackling this challenge?

If the answer to any of these questions is yes, it's time to step back into your comfort zone or productive discomfort zone. This gives you a chance to regroup, build your confidence, and approach the challenge with a more strategic mindset.

Fear Isn't Growth

The hustle culture often glorifies fear as a sign that you're growing. But the reality is, fear is not synonymous with growth. Growth happens when you're stretched, but not overwhelmed. It happens when you face challenges that push you to expand your capabilities, but that are still within your reach.

When you equate fear with growth, you risk putting yourself in situations where you're no longer learning, but simply struggling. Fear may be a natural part of life, but it should not be your constant companion in the pursuit of success. Growth requires a balance of challenge and control, and the fear zone robs you of that balance.

Expanding Comfort Without Entering Fear

The key to real growth is knowing how to expand your comfort zone without entering the fear zone. Here are a few strategies:

- Take Small, Measured Steps: Instead of making big leaps into unfamiliar territory, take smaller, controlled steps outside your comfort zone. This helps you stay in a state of productive discomfort, where you're challenged but not overwhelmed.
- Build a Support System: When venturing into new challenges, it helps to have a support system in place. Mentors, colleagues, or friends can provide guidance, encouragement, and feedback, making the transition

smoother and less fearful.

- Prepare and Plan: Fear often stems from a lack of preparation. Before stepping outside your comfort zone, make sure you have a clear plan and the resources you need to succeed. Being prepared reduces uncertainty and helps you stay confident in your ability to handle new challenges.
- Recognize Your Limits: It's important to know your own limits and recognize when you're pushing too far. Pushing boundaries is great—but pushing them too far, too fast can lead to burnout and fear. Understanding your limits allows you to grow in a sustainable, healthy way.

The Balance Between Comfort and Growth

The fear zone is a dangerous place for sustained growth. While stepping out of your comfort zone is important, doing so without preparation, strategy, or support can lead to overwhelm, burnout, and self-doubt. True growth happens not when you're paralyzed by fear, but when you expand your comfort zone gradually, pushing boundaries while staying in control.

Knowing the dangers of the fear zone helps you recognize when you're pushing too far and allows you to recalibrate. Growth requires a balance between challenge and comfort, and the key to sustainable success lies in expanding your comfort zone while avoiding the pitfalls of fear.

Leverage Your Comfort Zone

CHAPTER ELEVEN

Using Your Comfort Zone as a Strategic Base

The comfort zone is often misunderstood as a place where growth stagnates. However, when used wisely, it can be your most powerful tool for success. Rather than viewing your comfort zone as something to escape, you can use it as a strategic base—a stronghold from which you expand your skills, knowledge, and influence. Operating from this foundation allows you to grow in a way that's sustainable, purposeful, and aligned with your strengths.

The Comfort Zone: Your Zone of Excellence

Your comfort zone is not a barrier; it's a space where you operate at your best. It's where your skills are sharp, your confidence is high, and you have the clarity to make smart decisions. Think of it as your zone of excellence—a place where you are in control, and where you've mastered the necessary tools to succeed.

When you work within this zone, you can focus on refining and optimizing your strengths. You can also explore new opportunities from a position of confidence, making sure that your next steps are calculated and deliberate, rather than driven by fear or uncertainty. This approach keeps you grounded while still allowing you to push the boundaries of what you already know.

The Comfort Zone as a Launchpad

Rather than thinking of your comfort zone as a stagnant place, consider it a launchpad for growth. It's the space where you recharge, reflect, and regroup before making strategic moves. Just like elite athletes who perfect their skills through repetition before facing new competition, your comfort zone is where you sharpen your tools for future challenges.

By staying in this space of mastery, you're able to prepare yourself mentally, emotionally, and physically for the next step. Whether that step involves learning new skills, taking on bigger projects, or expanding your expertise, you're doing it with a solid foundation under your feet.

The key is not to abandon your comfort zone but to use it as a base from which you can expand your horizons. Growth doesn't have to mean stepping into chaos—it can mean systematically pushing the boundaries of what's familiar, while still relying on your comfort zone as your center of strength.

Strategic Growth: Expanding, Not Abandoning

Growth is often portrayed as a dramatic leap into the

unknown, but it doesn't have to be. Instead, think of growth as expanding your comfort zone rather than abandoning it. By pushing the edges of your comfort zone outward, you slowly incorporate new skills, knowledge, and experiences into your existing base.

This approach allows you to manage risk more effectively. Instead of jumping headfirst into an unfamiliar environment, you're gradually stretching your limits, moving into new challenges at a pace that feels manageable. This type of strategic growth minimizes the risk of overwhelm and burnout while maximizing your potential for long-term success.

Each time you expand your comfort zone, it becomes bigger. Your mastery grows, your confidence increases, and the areas in which you excel expand. Over time, you'll find that what was once outside your comfort zone is now comfortably within it, and you're ready to push the boundaries even further.

Recharging in Your Comfort Zone

Another critical benefit of using your comfort zone as a strategic base is that it provides a place to recharge. Growth and challenge require energy—both mental and emotional. While it's important to step into new experiences, constantly living in a state of discomfort is exhausting.

Your comfort zone allows you to regroup after tackling challenges outside of it. It's the place where you can reflect on your progress, process your experiences, and prepare for the next phase of growth. When used effectively, this recharging process is not about stagnation, but about ensuring that you have the energy and focus needed for sustained success.

Taking the time to recharge also prevents burnout. When you've stretched yourself too thin or taken on too many challenges at once, returning to your comfort zone allows you to regain balance and avoid the fatigue that often accompanies pushing too hard, too fast.

Building Confidence from a Position of Strength

One of the greatest advantages of operating from your comfort zone is that it builds confidence. Confidence isn't built from constant discomfort; it's built from mastering what you know and then gradually expanding from that mastery. When you make decisions from a position of strength, you can handle challenges with poise and clarity.

This doesn't mean avoiding new experiences, but rather ensuring that each new challenge builds upon your existing strengths. When you use your comfort zone as a base, you're not throwing yourself into the deep end—you're expanding into new territory with the confidence that comes from knowing you have a strong foundation to fall back on.

Confidence grows with competence. The more you refine your skills within your comfort zone, the more confident you become in your ability to handle bigger and more complex challenges. This cycle of confidence and competence reinforces your ability to grow strategically, without the fear and uncertainty that often accompanies stepping too far outside your comfort zone.

Navigating Challenges on Your Own Terms

When you operate from your comfort zone, you're in control of the pace and direction of your growth. You can decide when to push boundaries, when to retreat and recharge, and when to take on new challenges. This control is essential for sustainable growth.

Operating on your own terms means that you're not being forced into uncomfortable situations just for the sake of growth. Instead, you're strategically choosing the moments when stepping outside your comfort zone makes the most sense. You're growing on your terms, not on someone else's timeline or expectations.

This kind of growth is intentional, not reactionary. You're not reacting to external pressures or jumping into unknown situations without preparation. Instead, you're making thoughtful, calculated decisions that ensure you're growing in a way that aligns with your strengths, goals, and values.

Expanding Your Comfort Zone, Not Escaping It

The goal isn't to escape your comfort zone but to gradually expand it. When you do this, you're not abandoning your strengths or leaving behind what you've mastered. You're building on those strengths, expanding your mastery, and integrating new skills and experiences into your comfort zone.

Over time, what was once a challenge becomes part of your comfort zone. This process of expansion is sustainable and repeatable. You're not experiencing growth in sporadic bursts followed by periods of burnout or exhaustion. Instead, you're growing continuously, strategically pushing the boundaries of what's comfortable, while maintaining the confidence and clarity that comes from staying grounded in your strengths.

The Power of a Strategic Comfort Zone

Your comfort zone isn't something to escape—it's something to leverage. By using it as a strategic base, you can grow in a way that's intentional, controlled, and aligned with your strengths. Whether it's recharging after a challenge, expanding your skill set, or navigating new opportunities, your comfort zone provides the foundation from which you can achieve sustained success.

The key is to balance the safety of your comfort zone with the willingness to expand it. Growth doesn't have to mean chaos. By using your comfort zone strategically, you can create a cycle of mastery, confidence, and continuous growth.

CHAPTER TWELVE

Expanding the Boundaries Without Stepping into Chaos

The common advice to "step outside your comfort zone" is often taken to extremes, leading people to believe that the only way to grow is to venture far into unknown territory. While exploring new challenges is important, pushing yourself too far, too quickly can lead to chaos—where uncertainty, overwhelm, and fear take over. Instead, the key to sustainable growth lies in strategically expanding the boundaries of your comfort zone without diving into chaos.

Understanding Controlled Expansion

Growth doesn't have to be a dramatic leap into the unknown. It can—and often should—be a controlled expansion of what you already know and do well. Controlled expansion means pushing your limits incrementally, so that you are continuously improving without feeling overwhelmed.

When you expand the boundaries of your comfort zone in a controlled way, you give yourself time to adapt, reflect, and strengthen your new skills. This process allows for sustainable growth rather than growth that leads to stress, burnout, or panic. By taking small, measured steps, you can steadily increase your capacity without sacrificing the confidence and stability you've built within your comfort zone.

Avoiding the Chaos of the Fear Zone

When you push yourself too far outside your comfort zone, you risk entering the fear zone—a space where uncertainty, self-doubt, and stress dominate. In the fear zone, instead of growing, you're simply trying to survive. You're overwhelmed by new challenges and responsibilities, which can lead to anxiety, poor decision-making, and even paralysis.

Chaos in the fear zone creates a situation where you're reacting to stress rather than responding to challenges with clarity and confidence. This isn't productive growth—it's self-sabotage. Instead of thriving, you're just trying to cope. The goal of expanding your comfort zone isn't to abandon the stability you've built, but to carefully push the boundaries so that you're growing without losing control.

The Gradual Expansion Approach

The process of expanding your comfort zone should be gradual, with each new challenge integrated into the skills and strengths you've already developed. By taking small, manageable steps, you allow yourself time to reflect, adjust, and refine your approach before moving on to the next level of growth.

Here's how you can implement gradual expansion:

Set Small, Achievable Goals: Instead of taking on a huge challenge all at once, break it down into smaller, more manageable steps. For example, if you want to improve public speaking, start by speaking in front of a small group before addressing a large audience.

Focus on One Area at a Time: Trying to grow in too many areas at once can lead to chaos. Focus on expanding the boundaries of one skill or area before moving on to the next. This allows you to give your full attention to each area of growth.

Build on Existing Strengths: Expansion should build upon what you already know and do well. When you take on a new challenge, make sure it connects to your existing skill set. For example, if you're great at problem-solving but weak in leadership, start by leading a project where problem-solving is central, so you're still operating from a place of strength while learning a new skill.

Evaluate Progress Frequently: After each step, reflect on your progress and make any necessary adjustments. This reflection helps you learn from your experiences and identify any areas where you may need further growth or support. Regular evaluation also ensures you're expanding in a thoughtful, deliberate way rather than getting swept up in chaos.

Maintaining Control During Expansion

Control is the foundation of successful expansion. When you maintain control over your environment, emotions, and actions, you can stretch the limits of your comfort zone without losing stability. Here's how to maintain control during the expansion process:

- **Pace Yourself:** Growth isn't a race. Give yourself the time you need to master each step before moving on to the next. Pacing yourself ensures that you're not rushing through the process, which can lead to mistakes or overwhelm.
- **Create a Support System:** Don't go through expansion alone. Having mentors, colleagues, or friends who can offer guidance, encouragement, and constructive feedback can make the process more manageable. They can help you stay grounded and focused, preventing you from slipping into chaos.
- **Stay Organized:** Chaos often arises from a lack of organization. When you're expanding your comfort zone, keep your goals, steps, and milestones clearly defined. Use checklists, timelines, or any other tools that help you stay organized and on track. This organization keeps your progress structured, preventing the confusion that comes with disorganization.
- **Keep the Big Picture in Mind:** As you expand your boundaries, keep your long-term goals in focus. It's easy to get caught up in the challenges of the moment, but by reminding yourself of the bigger picture, you can stay motivated and avoid feeling overwhelmed by temporary difficulties.

Balancing Challenge with Stability

Expanding your comfort zone is about finding the right balance between challenge and stability. Too much challenge leads to chaos, while too much stability leads to stagnation. The sweet spot lies in maintaining enough stability to feel confident and grounded, while gradually increasing the level of challenge to foster growth.

This balance allows you to stay in control of your progress while still pushing yourself to achieve more. It's not about avoiding discomfort altogether—it's about ensuring that the discomfort you face is productive, not chaotic.

Learning from Each Expansion

Each time you push the boundaries of your comfort zone, it's an opportunity for learning. Rather than rushing from one challenge to the next, take time to reflect on each experience and identify what worked, what didn't, and how you can improve moving forward.

Reflection helps you build on your experiences, so that each time you expand your comfort zone, you're doing it more strategically. You'll also gain a better understanding of your limits, which helps you avoid overextending yourself and entering the chaos of the fear zone.

The Power of Gradual Mastery

By expanding your comfort zone gradually, you can build mastery over time. Mastery comes from repetition, refinement, and deliberate practice—none of which happen when you're constantly jumping from one chaotic challenge to another. Instead of chasing the thrill of the unknown, you're steadily growing, building on your strengths, and developing new skills in a way that sticks.

Each time you successfully expand your comfort zone, your new skills and experiences become part of your zone of mastery. Over time, you'll find that challenges that once seemed intimidating are now within your comfort zone, and you can take on even bigger opportunities without losing your footing.

Growth Without Chaos

Expanding the boundaries of your comfort zone doesn't have to mean diving into chaos. By taking a gradual, controlled approach to growth, you can push your limits in a way that is sustainable, purposeful, and aligned with your strengths. Strategic expansion allows you to avoid the pitfalls of the fear zone and maintain the confidence, clarity, and control needed for long-term success.

Remember, the goal isn't to abandon your comfort zone—it's to steadily stretch its boundaries so that what was once a challenge becomes a new part of your mastery. Growth doesn't have to be chaotic. When done intentionally, it's a process of expanding your strengths while staying grounded in stability.

The Smart Way to Step Outside While Staying Inside

CHAPTER THIRTEEN

How to Safely Expand Your Comfort Zone

Expanding your comfort zone is essential for growth, but it's crucial to do it safely and strategically to avoid burnout, fear, or chaos. The goal is not to leap into overwhelming situations but to stretch your limits gradually and deliberately. When done right, expanding your comfort zone can lead to sustained success and continuous learning without losing the stability that supports your progress.

Here's how you can safely expand your comfort zone while maintaining control and confidence:

1. Start with Small, Manageable Steps

Rather than jumping into drastic or unfamiliar challenges, start with small, manageable steps. The key is to introduce changes that challenge you just enough to push your boundaries but not so much that you feel overwhelmed or anxious.

For example, if public speaking is outside your comfort zone, you don't need to start with a keynote address in front of hundreds of people. Instead, begin by speaking in small groups or casual settings. Over time, as your confidence grows, you can take on larger audiences.

How to do it:

- Break down big challenges into smaller, more achievable goals.
- Focus on one aspect of the challenge at a time, such as improving a single skill rather than tackling everything at once.
- Gradually increase the difficulty as your confidence and competence grow.

2. Expand in Familiar Areas

When expanding your comfort zone, it helps to build on areas where you already have some expertise or confidence. This ensures that you're not stepping into completely unfamiliar territory but are expanding based on your existing strengths.

For instance, if you're a skilled writer, but marketing yourself is uncomfortable, start by writing content that promotes your work. You're still leveraging your writing skills while slowly learning the marketing side. This keeps the core of what you know intact while allowing you to stretch into new areas.

How to do it:

- Choose challenges that are adjacent to your strengths. This allows you to build on what you already know.

- Focus on areas where you feel secure and competent, then gradually branch out to related skills or tasks.

3. Set Clear, Measurable Goals

Expanding your comfort zone safely requires a clear sense of direction. Set measurable goals for yourself that define exactly what you want to achieve and by when. This helps you track your progress and stay focused, rather than getting lost in the uncertainty of a new challenge.

By breaking down larger objectives into smaller, measurable steps, you can ensure that each step outside your comfort zone is purposeful and attainable. This also gives you the opportunity to celebrate small wins, boosting your confidence along the way.

How to do it:

- Define clear, specific goals for each stage of your comfort zone expansion.
- Make your goals measurable so you can track progress (e.g., "Speak to a group of 10 people by the end of the month").
- Set a timeline to keep yourself accountable, but allow flexibility if needed.

4. Use Reflection to Learn and Adapt

One of the safest ways to expand your comfort zone is through regular reflection. After each new challenge or step outside your comfort zone, take time to reflect on what worked, what didn't, and what you learned. This helps you avoid repeating mistakes and ensures that each new step is a learning experience.

Reflection helps you adapt and refine your approach, ensuring that you're moving forward with insight and intention. It also allows you to evaluate whether the challenge was too overwhelming or if you can stretch further the next time.

How to do it:

- After each experience, ask yourself questions like: "What went well?" "What was difficult?" and "How can I improve next time?"
- Keep a journal or notes of your reflections to track your progress and see how far you've come.
- Use your reflections to adjust your approach for future challenges, ensuring that each step feels manageable and meaningful.

5. Surround Yourself with Support

Expanding your comfort zone can feel intimidating, but you don't have to do it alone. Having a support system—whether it's mentors, friends, or colleagues—can make the process more manageable. These people can offer guidance, encouragement, and constructive feedback as you venture into new territory.

A support system provides reassurance, reminding you that you have people in your corner who believe in your abilities. They can also help you see blind spots or offer solutions to challenges that might feel overwhelming when faced alone.

How to do it:

- Seek out mentors who have been through similar growth experiences and can offer advice.
- Share your goals with a trusted friend or colleague who can keep you accountable.
- Join groups or communities of like-minded individuals who are also working on expanding their comfort zones.

6. Celebrate Small Wins

Recognizing your progress is essential for maintaining motivation. When you're working to expand your comfort zone, every small victory is a step toward greater growth. Celebrating these wins—no matter how small—reinforces your belief in your ability to stretch and succeed.

Acknowledging small wins also helps to prevent feelings of overwhelm. It reminds you that progress is happening, even if the steps feel incremental. This positive reinforcement boosts your confidence, making the next step easier.

How to do it:

- Celebrate each milestone, no matter how small—whether it's completing a task or overcoming a minor fear.
- Reward yourself for stepping out of your comfort zone in meaningful ways.
- Use your achievements as fuel for your next challenge.

7. Pace Yourself to Prevent Burnout

One of the biggest mistakes people make when trying to expand their comfort zone is pushing themselves too hard, too fast. This can lead to burnout and leave you feeling discouraged. The key is to pace yourself, allowing time for recovery between challenges.

Growth is a marathon, not a sprint. Expanding your comfort zone doesn't happen overnight—it's a process that requires patience and persistence. Make sure you're balancing periods of challenge with time to rest and recharge in your comfort zone. This ensures that you're not depleting your energy or enthusiasm.

How to do it:

- Set a pace that feels sustainable, allowing for periods of rest and reflection between challenges.
- Avoid taking on too many new challenges at once. Focus on one area of growth at a time.
- Be mindful of your energy levels and mental health, ensuring that you're not pushing yourself too hard.

8. Accept That Setbacks Are Part of the Process

No growth journey is without its setbacks. When expanding your comfort zone, it's normal to encounter challenges, failures, or obstacles that slow your progress. The key is to see these setbacks as part of the learning process rather than as signs of failure.

Every setback offers valuable lessons, helping you refine your approach and develop greater resilience. By accepting that setbacks are inevitable, you can maintain your motivation and keep moving forward with confidence.

How to do it:

- Embrace setbacks as learning opportunities, not failures.
- Analyze what went wrong, and use those insights to adjust your approach moving forward.
- Stay patient and persistent, knowing that growth takes time and effort.

Expanding Safely for Lasting Growth

Expanding your comfort zone safely doesn't mean avoiding challenges—it means approaching them with strategy, patience, and intention. By taking small steps, building on existing strengths, and reflecting on your progress, you can push your boundaries without feeling overwhelmed or losing control.

The process of growth is about gradually stretching what you know, incorporating new experiences into your comfort zone, and celebrating each success along the way. With the right mindset and support system, you can continue expanding your comfort zone safely and sustainably, ensuring lasting personal and professional development.

CHAPTER FOURTEEN

Identifying New Arenas of Success

One of the most powerful ways to grow without abandoning your comfort zone is by identifying new arenas of success that align with your existing strengths. These new areas can provide fresh challenges and opportunities while still allowing you to leverage the expertise and mastery you've already developed. Expanding into new arenas doesn't mean stepping into chaos—it means building on what you already know and finding new ways to apply your skills strategically.

By identifying new arenas of success, you can expand your horizons while maintaining control, confidence, and focus.

1. Leverage Existing Strengths

The best new arenas for growth are those that build on the strengths you've already mastered. Rather than diving into an entirely unfamiliar domain, seek out areas that allow you to use your current skills, knowledge, and experience in new ways. This approach not only ensures that you're not starting from scratch but also sets you up for quicker wins and sustained success.

For example, if you're a great communicator in your current role, a new arena of success might involve leadership or mentorship roles where communication is key. You're not stepping into a completely foreign territory, but you're applying your strengths in a new and impactful way.

How to do it:

- Identify your core strengths—whether it's problem-solving, creativity, leadership, or technical skills—and think about how they could apply to different roles, industries, or projects.
- Explore adjacent fields or responsibilities within your current domain where your strengths can provide a competitive advantage.
- Seek out roles, projects, or challenges where your existing expertise is valued but you can still learn and grow.

2. Find Cross-Domain Opportunities

Another powerful way to identify new arenas of success is by looking for cross-domain opportunities—situations where you can combine your skills from one field with the needs of another. Cross-domain thinking allows you to bridge gaps between industries or roles, creating unique solutions or innovations.

For example, if you have experience in data analysis but also have a passion for marketing, you could identify an arena where data-driven marketing is crucial. This cross-domain approach allows you to blend your expertise in different fields and find success in a space where your combined skill set is rare and valuable.

How to do it:

- Look for intersections between different fields or industries where your combination of skills could be uniquely valuable.
- Explore opportunities where knowledge from one domain can be applied innovatively in another.
- Network with professionals in adjacent industries to understand where cross-domain expertise is in demand.

3. Explore Emerging Trends and Technologies

New arenas of success often emerge in response to new trends and technologies. By staying informed about developments in your industry or areas of interest, you can identify new opportunities before they become widely recognized. This gives you a head start in mastering a new field while leveraging your existing expertise.

For example, if you're in the tech industry and you notice growing demand for skills related to artificial intelligence, blockchain, or cybersecurity, you can position yourself in these emerging areas. Expanding your knowledge in these fields allows you to be at the forefront of innovation, giving you an edge while still building on the foundation you already have.

How to do it:

- Stay informed by following industry news, attending conferences, and networking with thought leaders.
- Identify emerging trends that align with your interests and strengths, and start building your knowledge or skills in those areas.
- Look for areas where your expertise can intersect with new trends or technologies, allowing you to apply what you know in innovative ways.

4. Seek Strategic Growth Within Your Industry

Sometimes, the most powerful new arena of success can be found within your existing industry by taking on new roles or expanding your influence. Instead of switching industries or taking on entirely new challenges, consider exploring leadership opportunities, specialized roles, or strategic projects within your current domain.

For example, if you've been successful in a technical role, a new arena for success could be moving into project management, where you apply your technical knowledge while also developing leadership and organizational skills. This approach allows you to grow without abandoning your expertise.

How to do it:

- Identify growth opportunities within your current field, such as leadership roles, specialized projects, or cross-departmental initiatives.
- Consider lateral moves that allow you to develop new skills while still working in your area of expertise.

- Seek out mentorship or additional training that can prepare you for more strategic roles within your industry.

5. Align with Your Passions and Values

New arenas of success don't always have to be purely professional—they can also be aligned with your personal passions and values. When you find opportunities that resonate with what truly motivates you, you're more likely to excel because the work feels meaningful and fulfilling.

For instance, if you're passionate about sustainability, you might seek out roles or projects that allow you to contribute to environmental efforts. This could involve working with green technologies, sustainable business practices, or corporate social responsibility programs. These new arenas can give you a sense of purpose while also allowing you to apply your skills in a way that feels personally rewarding.

How to do it:

- Reflect on your personal passions, values, and long-term goals, and think about how they align with potential new arenas of success.
- Seek out roles, projects, or industries that resonate with your values, even if they require you to learn new skills along the way.
- Explore volunteer opportunities, side projects, or collaborations that allow you to work on things you're passionate about while still leveraging your core strengths.

6. Identify High-Growth Areas

One of the most effective ways to expand into new arenas is to target high-growth areas where opportunities are abundant, and competition is still limited. By moving into areas that are experiencing rapid growth, you can position yourself as an early adopter and leader in that field, giving you a competitive edge.

High-growth areas can vary by industry, but they often involve emerging technologies, shifting market demands, or societal trends. These areas offer significant opportunities for advancement as they are often underexplored and evolving quickly. By positioning yourself strategically in these spaces, you can capitalize on the momentum while still applying your core competencies.

How to do it:

- Research high-growth sectors in your industry or related fields, such as renewable energy, fintech, e-commerce, or health tech.
- Evaluate the skills and expertise needed in these areas, and start building knowledge to stay ahead of the curve.
- Look for high-growth companies or projects where you can contribute and grow alongside the industry's rapid expansion.

7. Look for Areas Where Your Experience is Rare

Sometimes the best new arenas of success are those where

your unique experience is rare and highly valued. This could involve targeting niche industries or specialized roles where the combination of skills and expertise you bring is in high demand but hard to find.

For example, if you have deep expertise in a specific technology or methodology that's not widely adopted yet, you can carve out a niche for yourself as an expert in that area. By identifying arenas where your expertise is scarce, you can create opportunities for leadership, consulting, or innovation.

How to do it:

- Identify industries or roles where your skills and experience are relatively rare or underrepresented.
- Look for niche markets where specialized knowledge is needed but not widely available.
- Position yourself as a subject matter expert in those areas, offering unique value that sets you apart from the competition.

8. Consider Global or Remote Opportunities

In today's increasingly interconnected world, new arenas of success aren't limited to your immediate geographic location. Consider global or remote opportunities where your skills could be in demand in different markets or regions. This can expand your options and introduce you to new challenges without requiring a complete career shift.

For instance, if you have expertise in a specialized field, you might find that companies or clients in other countries or time zones are in need of your services. Remote work or global opportunities can also introduce you to different cultures and perspectives, further expanding your comfort zone and network.

How to do it:

- Explore remote or international opportunities that allow you to apply your expertise in new markets.
- Research industries and roles that are experiencing growth in different parts of the world.
- Leverage global networks and platforms to connect with international companies, clients, or collaborators.

Strategic Expansion into New Arenas

Identifying new arenas of success doesn't have to mean leaving behind what you've mastered—it's about building on your strengths and finding new ways to apply them. By exploring adjacent fields, cross-domain opportunities, and emerging trends, you can strategically expand your comfort zone into areas where your expertise is valued and growth is sustainable.

The key is to seek out arenas that align with your existing skills while offering room for innovation, development, and fulfillment. With a thoughtful approach, you can unlock new paths to success while maintaining the control and confidence that come from leveraging your comfort zone.

Control Your Narrative

CHAPTER FIFTEEN

Staying in Control of Your Story While Others Struggle

Today's world that is fast-paced and high-pressure, it's easy to feel like you need to constantly push yourself into uncomfortable situations to keep up. However, there's an overlooked power in staying in control of your own story while others struggle to navigate the chaos of theirs. By maintaining focus within your comfort zone, you can shape your path with clarity and purpose, even as those around you may feel lost or overwhelmed by chasing external validation or trends.

The Power of Self-Control

At the heart of personal and professional success is self-control—the ability to manage your actions, emotions, and decisions from a place of strength. When you operate within your comfort zone, you maintain control over your narrative, making conscious, deliberate choices that align with your goals and values. Instead of being swayed by external pressures or the latest trends, you stay true to your direction, moving forward with intention.

While others may feel the need to constantly reinvent themselves or react to external challenges, staying in control of your story allows you to stay grounded. You are not reacting out of fear, desperation, or uncertainty. Instead, you are proactively writing your own narrative—deciding when to expand, when to step back, and when to take calculated risks that align with your long-term vision.

Remaining True to Your Goals

Many people struggle because they chase goals that aren't truly their own. Whether it's societal expectations, workplace pressures, or comparison to others, the pursuit of someone else's definition of success can lead to frustration, burnout, or dissatisfaction. By staying in control of your story, you ensure that the goals you're working toward are authentic to you.

This doesn't mean avoiding challenges or new opportunities. It means making sure that each challenge you take on serves a purpose in your broader life plan. When you're clear on your goals, you can confidently say no to distractions that don't align with your priorities, while also recognizing the right moments to push your limits.

How to Stay True to Your Goals:

- Clarify Your Vision: Take time to define what success means to you—professionally and personally. Ensure that your goals reflect your values, interests, and aspirations, rather than external expectations.

- Reassess Regularly: Goals can evolve. Periodically reassess your objectives to ensure they still align with who you are and where you want to go.
- Filter Out Noise: Not every opportunity or trend is meant for you. Stay focused on what matters most, and don't get distracted by things that don't contribute to your long-term vision.

The Illusion of Constant Struggle

There's a common misconception that constant struggle equals growth. While it's true that challenges can help you grow, not all struggle is productive. Many people push themselves into situations of unnecessary discomfort, believing that constant hardship is the only path to success. However, this often leads to burnout, frustration, and feelings of inadequacy.

By staying in control of your story, you recognize that not every battle is yours to fight. You don't need to constantly be on the edge of discomfort to achieve success. Instead, you can focus on strategic growth—expanding your comfort zone gradually, while maintaining the clarity and energy needed to keep moving forward. This approach allows you to grow without losing yourself in the process.

The Real Power: Consistency Over Chaos

While others may find themselves struggling in a cycle of chaos, chasing the next big thing, or trying to keep up with shifting demands, you can find power in consistency. Consistency doesn't mean stagnation—it means deliberate, thoughtful progress that builds on your strengths and long-term goals.

Consistency allows you to create a sustainable rhythm of growth. Instead of leaping from one chaotic challenge to the next, you're focusing on refining and improving what you do best, while strategically expanding your skill set over time. This steady progress might not seem as dramatic as constant hustle, but it leads to real mastery and long-term success.

Why Consistency Wins:

- Builds Mastery: Repeated actions within your comfort zone allow you to refine and perfect your skills, leading to deep expertise.
- Avoids Burnout: Consistent, steady progress is sustainable and prevents the exhaustion that comes from constant chaos.
- Increases Confidence: When you're consistently working within your zone of excellence, your confidence grows, enabling you to take on larger challenges with greater ease.

Controlling the Narrative in Uncertainty

One of the most valuable aspects of staying in control of your story is how it helps you navigate uncertainty. When the world around you feels chaotic—whether due to economic shifts, industry changes, or personal challenges—those who have control over their narrative can remain calm, focused, and adaptive. Instead of getting swept up in the uncertainty, you have the clarity to assess the situation, adjust your strategy, and move forward with confidence.

In contrast, those who operate without control often feel overwhelmed by uncertainty. They are reactive, making decisions based on panic or fear. By maintaining a clear sense of purpose and direction, you can stay on course, even in times of change.

How to Control the Narrative:

Stick to Your Plan, but Stay Flexible: While it's important to have a plan, flexibility is key. When unexpected challenges arise, adapt without abandoning your long-term goals.

Stay Calm in the Face of Chaos: Use your comfort zone as a base of strength during uncertain times. Take a step back, assess the situation, and make decisions from a place of calm, not fear.

Focus on What You Can Control: You can't control everything happening around you, but you can control your actions, mindset, and approach to challenges.

Using Your Comfort Zone as a Competitive Advantage

While others struggle to reinvent themselves in every new situation, you can use your comfort zone as a competitive advantage. Operating from a space of mastery allows you to perform at your best without the distractions of constant change or chaos. When others are stretched thin trying to navigate the unknown, you can deliver results with precision and confidence because you've built a strong foundation.

This doesn't mean avoiding challenges—it means facing them from a place of strength. When you expand your comfort zone deliberately, you're better equipped to handle new situations without losing your focus. Your comfort zone becomes the platform from which you launch into new arenas, explore new opportunities, and grow with purpose.

The Advantage of Mastery:

- Focus on Refinement: While others are struggling with basics, you're refining and perfecting your skills, which gives you a significant edge.
- Confidence in Execution: You're able to execute tasks with a level of confidence that comes from deep expertise, making you a reliable leader in your field.
- Stability Amidst Change: While others may be thrown off by changes or trends, you maintain stability, ensuring your performance remains high even in times of flux.

Write Your Own Narrative

Staying in control of your story while others struggle doesn't mean avoiding challenges or resisting growth. It means strategically expanding your comfort zone, making deliberate decisions, and maintaining a clear sense of purpose. While others chase external validation or react to chaos, you can move forward with clarity, focus, and confidence—building a narrative of success that is uniquely yours.

By controlling your narrative, you ensure that you're not just surviving the pressures of the outside world but thriving on your terms. Success doesn't require constant discomfort or struggle. It requires a balanced approach that leverages your strengths, expands your comfort zone strategically, and maintains control over your personal and professional journey.

CHAPTER SIXTEEN

How Comfort Creates Confidence and Command

One of the most overlooked aspects of success is the role that comfort plays in building both confidence and a sense of command over your life, work, and decisions. While society often glorifies the hustle, discomfort, and constant striving, the truth is that comfort—when properly understood and leveraged—can be the foundation for long-term confidence, authority, and leadership.

When you operate from a place of comfort, you're not just at ease—you're in control. You know the terrain, you trust your skills, and this breeds the kind of confidence that others notice and respect. Over time, comfort leads to command: the ability to take decisive actions, make sound judgments, and lead with authority, all while staying calm and centered.

1. Comfort as the Foundation of Confidence

Confidence is often built through mastery—the repeated

practice and refinement of a skill or craft. Your comfort zone is where you develop that mastery. It's the space where you've practiced enough to feel competent, where your actions come naturally, and where you perform with ease. The more you practice and refine your skills within your comfort zone, the more confident you become in your ability to execute those skills in any situation.

When you're comfortable with what you know, your actions are backed by a deep sense of trust in your abilities. This trust is the foundation of confidence. You're not second-guessing yourself, and you're not constantly looking for external validation because you know you can deliver results. This self-assurance is what sets successful people apart from those who are constantly scrambling to prove themselves.

How Comfort Builds Confidence:

- Repetition and Mastery: The more you practice within your comfort zone, the more proficient you become, leading to increased self-confidence.
- Predictable Success: Operating from your comfort zone allows you to anticipate outcomes and challenges, giving you the confidence to handle situations with ease.
- Strengthens Self-Belief: As you continue to succeed within your comfort zone, your self-belief grows, and you become more confident in your ability to tackle even bigger challenges.

2. Command Comes from Stability

The concept of "command" isn't just about leadership; it's about having control over your environment and decisions. When you operate from a place of comfort, you're able to maintain a sense of stability that allows you to think clearly, act decisively, and remain composed under pressure. Comfort offers you the ability to stay grounded when others might be reacting impulsively to challenges.

This stability leads to a greater sense of command because you're not overwhelmed by uncertainty. You know your strengths, you trust your instincts, and you have a deep understanding of the terrain you're navigating. Instead of constantly adapting to unfamiliar environments, you're directing the flow of your actions with precision and purpose.

Command is rooted in the idea that you are in control, not just of yourself but of the situations you encounter. By staying in your comfort zone, you give yourself the mental space to make thoughtful, deliberate decisions rather than reactive ones. Over time, this steady approach builds your leadership presence and your ability to guide others confidently.

How Comfort Leads to Command:

- Clarity in Decision-Making: When you're in control of your environment, you make decisions from a place of stability, not stress or panic.
- Calm Under Pressure: Comfort creates mental clarity, allowing you to maintain composure and command, even in challenging situations.
- Consistency of Actions: Operating from a place of comfort ensures you can act consistently and confidently, making others trust your leadership and

judgment.

3. Building Authority Through Confidence

People gravitate toward those who exude confidence. When you operate from a place of comfort, the confidence you project is genuine. It's not based on bravado or faking it until you make it—it's rooted in your actual mastery and competence. This kind of confidence leads to authority because others recognize that you know what you're doing and trust you to lead or make important decisions.

Your comfort zone, when properly expanded and cultivated, becomes the space from which you can lead with authority. As you continue to refine your skills, achieve consistent results, and demonstrate calm command in various situations, others begin to look to you as a source of expertise and leadership. This is how you build authority naturally—not through force or ego, but through consistent, confident performance that others respect.

How Comfort Creates Authority:

- Earned Respect: Confidence that comes from comfort and mastery leads to earned respect, as others see that your expertise is backed by real results.
- Influence Over Others: People naturally gravitate toward those who are calm, composed, and confident, giving you more influence in both personal and professional spheres.
- Leadership Presence: When you consistently operate from a place of comfort and confidence, you naturally take on a leadership role, even if it's informal because

others trust your judgment.

4. Operating with Precision and Control

One of the key benefits of comfort is that it allows you to operate with precision. When you know your environment well, when you've mastered the necessary skills, and when you've refined your approach through repetition, you can perform tasks with a high level of accuracy and control. This precision is what gives you an edge in high-pressure situations where others may falter.

When you're operating outside your comfort zone, it's easy to make mistakes or lose focus because you're unfamiliar with the challenges you're facing. However, when you stay within or near your comfort zone, you can maintain complete control over your actions. This precision leads to more consistent results, which in turn, reinforces your confidence and command over your environment.

How Comfort Leads to Precision and Control:

- Refined Skills: Through repetition and practice, your actions become more precise, allowing you to perform tasks with greater efficiency and effectiveness.
- Predictability: Comfort allows you to anticipate outcomes, helping you make better decisions and maintain control over situations.
- Consistency: When you operate from a place of comfort, your performance is more consistent, which builds trust in your abilities both from yourself and others.

5. Expanding Comfort Creates Expanding Confidence

The more you expand your comfort zone, the more confident and in command you become. Each time you push the boundaries of your comfort zone, you stretch your capabilities without losing the control and stability you've built. This gradual expansion ensures that you're growing at a sustainable pace, and with each new skill or challenge you master, your comfort zone—and your confidence—grows.

As your comfort zone expands, so does your sphere of influence and authority. You're no longer just commanding the space you once mastered—you're continuously enlarging that space to include new areas of success. This gives you a competitive edge because you're always growing, but doing so in a way that doesn't overwhelm or destabilize you.

How Expanding Comfort Expands Confidence:

- Strategic Growth: Expanding your comfort zone strategically allows you to build confidence gradually, ensuring that you stay in control of your growth.
- Bigger Wins: As you expand, you take on bigger challenges, achieve more significant successes, and further reinforce your sense of command.
- Continuous Mastery: By consistently pushing the boundaries of your comfort zone, you build deeper expertise and maintain the confidence needed to lead with authority.

The Power of Comfort in Creating Confidence and

Command

Contrary to popular belief, comfort isn't the enemy of growth—it's the foundation of confidence and command. By staying within or near your comfort zone, you build a stable base that allows you to grow strategically, make decisions with clarity, and operate with precision. This approach leads to deep-seated confidence, a sense of command over your environment, and ultimately, the ability to lead with authority and influence.

Comfort creates the space for sustainable success by allowing you to refine your skills, build self-trust, and act with consistency. Over time, the confidence that comes from comfort leads to an undeniable command—both over your own life and in the eyes of others. The key is to recognize that comfort, when used strategically, is not about complacency; it's about creating the conditions for mastery, growth, and leadership.

Forget the Hustle Hype

CHAPTER SEVENTEEN

Why the "Discomfort" Mantra is Overrated

We've all heard the popular mantra: "Growth only happens outside your comfort zone." It's been repeated by motivational speakers, self-help books, and hustle culture advocates for years. The message is clear: to succeed, you must constantly seek discomfort. However, this idea—while well-intentioned—is often oversimplified and can even be counterproductive. The notion that discomfort is the only path to growth is overrated and overlooks the importance of strategy, stability, and the value of comfort.

Growth doesn't always require discomfort. In fact, real, sustainable growth often happens in a balance between challenge and comfort, where you can expand your capabilities while still operating from a place of confidence and control.

1. Discomfort Doesn't Always Lead to Growth

The belief that stepping into discomfort automatically leads to growth is fundamentally flawed. Discomfort, in itself, is not a guarantee of progress. While it can introduce new challenges and experiences, growth doesn't happen just because you're uncomfortable—it happens when you are able to learn, adapt, and apply new skills in a way that improves your performance or knowledge.

Simply being uncomfortable can often lead to stress, anxiety, and burnout rather than meaningful development. When you're constantly in a state of discomfort, your energy and focus are spent on surviving the experience, rather than mastering new skills or improving existing ones. In other words, discomfort without purpose or strategy is just chaos.

Why Discomfort Alone Isn't Enough:

- Survival Mode vs. Mastery: When you're overwhelmed by discomfort, your brain is in survival mode, making it difficult to learn or grow meaningfully.
- Random Challenge: Discomfort without a clear goal or structure leads to random challenges, which may not be aligned with your long-term success or personal development.
- Burnout Risk: Constant discomfort can drain your mental, emotional, and physical energy, leading to burnout instead of growth.

2. Growth Happens Through Mastery, Not Just Discomfort

The key to lasting growth is mastery, not simply pushing yourself into unfamiliar situations. Mastery is built through repetition, refinement, and deep understanding—none of which can be achieved if you're constantly jumping from one uncomfortable situation to the next.

When you stay within or near your comfort zone, you have the mental and emotional capacity to focus on honing your skills, building deeper expertise, and making steady, incremental progress. This approach creates a foundation of competence and confidence, allowing you to expand your abilities in a strategic, sustainable way.

Mastery as the Real Driver of Growth:

- Repetition Leads to Mastery: Practicing and refining your skills in a stable environment allows you to achieve higher levels of performance.
- Clarity and Focus: Comfort allows you to focus on improving key skills without the distraction of constant stress or fear.
- Incremental Progress: Rather than seeking constant discomfort, growth through mastery happens gradually, ensuring long-term improvement.

3. The Myth of Constant Hustle

The discomfort mantra often goes hand-in-hand with the glorification of constant hustle—the idea that success comes from working harder, longer, and always pushing beyond your limits. However, this mindset can lead to unhealthy work habits, burnout, and a lack of balance in both your personal and professional life.

Real success doesn't require being in a constant state of discomfort or hustle. Instead, it comes from working smarter, knowing when to push and when to rest, and focusing on growth in areas where you can make the most impact. Constant hustle may sound heroic, but it's often inefficient and unsustainable.

Why Constant Hustle Doesn't Work:

- Burnout Over Time: Continuous hustle and discomfort lead to exhaustion and eventually burnout, making long-term success difficult to maintain.
- Diminished Returns: As you push harder without breaks, the quality of your work often declines, and the growth you achieve is less effective.
- Sacrificing Well-Being: Prioritizing hustle over balance often means sacrificing your health, relationships, and mental well-being—none of which contribute to meaningful, sustainable success.

4. Comfort Doesn't Mean Stagnation

One of the biggest misconceptions about the comfort zone is that it equals stagnation. But comfort isn't the absence of growth—it's a strong foundation from which you can build. When you operate in your comfort zone, you're not avoiding challenges; you're creating a stable environment where you can explore, practice, and refine your skills.

Comfort provides the clarity and focus you need to approach new challenges thoughtfully, without the chaos that comes from operating in constant discomfort. It's in this space of comfort that you can make strategic decisions about how to expand, where to push your boundaries, and when to take risks that align with your goals.

Why Comfort Supports Growth:

- Base of Strength: Comfort allows you to operate from a place of strength, where you have the mental bandwidth to take on challenges effectively.
- Strategic Growth: Comfort provides the clarity needed to make smart decisions about when and how to step outside your zone.
- Confidence Builder: Mastery within your comfort zone builds confidence, making it easier to tackle bigger challenges over time.

5. Discomfort is Only Valuable When it's Strategic

While discomfort can lead to growth, it must be approached strategically. Random discomfort doesn't lead to meaningful improvement, but purposeful challenges—those that align with your goals and build on your strengths—do. The key is to approach discomfort with intention and a clear understanding of what you want to achieve.

By strategically pushing the boundaries of your comfort zone, you expand it in a sustainable way. This doesn't mean throwing yourself into chaotic or overwhelming situations—it means gradually introducing new challenges that stretch your abilities while still allowing you to maintain control. This approach ensures that discomfort leads to growth, not frustration.

How to Make Discomfort Productive:

- Align with Goals: Only step into discomfort that aligns with your long-term goals and growth objectives.

- Expand Gradually: Push the boundaries of your comfort zone in small, manageable steps, rather than making huge, risky leaps.
- Reflection and Learning: After stepping into discomfort, reflect on what you learned, what worked, and how you can improve next time.

6. True Growth Requires Balance, Not Extremes

The discomfort mantra often implies that you're either in your comfort zone (and not growing) or you're outside of it (and growing). This black-and-white thinking ignores the nuanced nature of real growth. The truth is, growth happens when you find the right balance between comfort and challenge—between stability and risk.

Too much comfort can lead to complacency, but too much discomfort can lead to burnout. The real key to success is understanding when to push and when to recharge. By balancing comfort and discomfort, you can achieve sustained growth that doesn't sacrifice your well-being or long-term success.

The Importance of Balance:

- Avoiding Extremes: Success doesn't require extremes of either comfort or discomfort. The best growth happens in the middle, where you're challenged but still in control.
- Sustainable Success: Balance ensures that you can continue growing without risking burnout or loss of motivation.

- Holistic Growth: Finding balance allows for growth in all areas of life—personal, professional, and emotional—without sacrificing one for the other.

Moving Beyond the Discomfort Mantra

The discomfort mantra is often overrated because it simplifies the complex nature of growth. While discomfort can lead to growth, it's not the only path—nor is it always the best one. Real, sustainable success happens when you balance comfort and challenge, allowing you to expand your capabilities in a strategic, thoughtful way.

By operating from a place of comfort, you can build the confidence, clarity, and mastery needed to grow without unnecessary struggle. Discomfort has its place, but only when approached with intention and purpose. In the end, the goal is not to abandon your comfort zone entirely, but to expand it in a way that leads to lasting success.

CHAPTER EIGHTEEN

Embracing Comfort as a Path to Sustained Success

In a world where hustle culture and constant discomfort are often glorified, the idea of embracing comfort might seem counterintuitive. However, comfort—when used strategically—can be the foundation for sustained success. Rather than avoiding it or seeing it as a sign of stagnation, comfort can provide the stability, clarity, and confidence needed to achieve long-term growth and fulfillment.

Comfort is not the enemy of success. It's a powerful tool for mastering your skills, making deliberate decisions, and expanding your potential in a sustainable, controlled way. By embracing comfort as part of your strategy, you set yourself up for success that is not only achievable but also enduring.

1. Comfort Provides Stability for Long-Term Growth

One of the most important advantages of operating within your comfort zone is that it provides a strong sense of stability. This stability allows you to focus deeply on your craft, improve your skills, and refine your approach without being distracted by constant external pressures. Instead of constantly facing new, unpredictable challenges, you can concentrate on honing what you know, getting better with each repetition.

Stability doesn't mean staying stagnant—it means creating a solid foundation from which you can build. In this stable environment, you can take calculated risks and push boundaries in a way that leads to growth, not chaos. You're not abandoning your comfort zone but expanding it incrementally, ensuring that your progress is sustainable over time.

Why Stability is Key:

- Consistent Progress: A stable environment allows for consistent, focused progress, which leads to mastery over time.
- Foundation for Exploration: Stability gives you the confidence to explore new areas without losing your sense of control.
- Predictable Success: By working from a stable base, you increase the predictability of success, reducing the risk of failure or burnout.

2. Comfort Fuels Confidence

Confidence is not built from constant discomfort; it's built from mastery and competence—both of which come from operating within your comfort zone. When you're comfortable, you're not second-guessing yourself or reacting to unfamiliar situations. Instead, you're leveraging your expertise and strengths, which boosts your confidence.

The more comfortable you are with your skills, the more confident you become in your ability to handle new challenges. This confidence allows you to take calculated risks when it matters most, pushing the boundaries of your comfort zone without feeling overwhelmed. Confidence derived from comfort is not fleeting; it's rooted in real mastery and experience, making it a powerful asset for sustained success.

How Comfort Builds Confidence:

- Repetition and Mastery: Comfort allows you to repeat and refine your skills, leading to deeper competence and increased confidence.
- Trust in Yourself: When you operate from a place of comfort, you trust your instincts and decisions, which empowers you to take on challenges with assurance.
- Controlled Growth: Confidence grows when you expand your comfort zone in a controlled, strategic way, knowing that you have a strong foundation to rely on.

3. Comfort Creates Clarity

Operating within your comfort zone provides a level of clarity that is hard to achieve when you're constantly in discomfort or stress. When you're comfortable, you can see things clearly—your goals, your progress, and the steps you need to take to achieve success. This clarity allows for better decision-making and ensures that you're moving forward with purpose and intention.

In contrast, constant discomfort often clouds your judgment. When you're overwhelmed by uncertainty, it's difficult to focus on long-term goals or think strategically. Embracing comfort gives you the mental space to step back, assess your progress, and make thoughtful decisions that align with your overall vision.

Why Clarity Matters:

- Purposeful Action: Clarity helps you take purposeful, intentional steps toward your goals, rather than reacting impulsively to challenges.
- Better Decision-Making: When your mind is clear, you can make decisions based on logic and strategy, rather than fear or pressure.
- Goal Alignment: Comfort provides the clarity needed to ensure that your actions align with your long-term goals, not just short-term demands.

4. Sustained Success Requires Balance, Not Extremes

The belief that success requires constant discomfort is a myth. True, sustained success is built on balance—between challenge and rest, growth and reflection, pushing boundaries and staying grounded. By embracing comfort, you create the balance needed to ensure that your growth is sustainable over time.

When you focus exclusively on discomfort, you risk burning out, losing motivation, or making reckless decisions. However, when you balance moments of challenge with periods of comfort, you can recharge, reflect, and prepare for the next step forward. This balanced approach keeps you energized, focused, and capable of achieving success that lasts.

Why Balance is Key:

- Prevents Burnout: Embracing comfort allows for necessary rest and recovery, preventing the burnout that often comes from constant hustle and discomfort.
- Sustainable Growth: Balance ensures that your growth is sustainable, allowing you to make steady progress without risking exhaustion or overwhelm.
- Holistic Success: A balanced approach allows you to succeed in all areas of life, not just work, by ensuring that you take care of your mental, physical, and emotional well-being.

5. Expanding Comfort for Continuous Growth

Embracing comfort doesn't mean staying static. It means using your comfort zone as a base to expand your skills, knowledge, and influence. Instead of leaping into chaos, you push the boundaries of your comfort zone strategically, ensuring that each step forward is controlled and intentional.

Each time you expand your comfort zone, you integrate new skills, experiences, and challenges into your existing strengths. Over time, what once felt difficult or uncomfortable becomes part of your new comfort zone. This approach to growth is sustainable and ensures that you're not just growing, but mastering new areas while maintaining your confidence and stability.

How to Expand Comfort for Growth:

- Gradual Expansion: Push the boundaries of your comfort zone in small, manageable steps, rather than making drastic leaps.
- Build on Strengths: Focus on expanding areas where you already have competence, ensuring that growth is aligned with your strengths.
- Reflect and Integrate: After each new challenge, reflect on your progress and integrate what you've learned into your comfort zone, making it a foundation for future growth.

6. Comfort Supports Strategic Risk-Taking

One of the greatest advantages of embracing comfort is that it allows you to take strategic risks from a place of strength. When you operate from comfort, you have a clear sense of your abilities, your limitations, and the opportunities that align with your goals. This self-awareness enables you to take calculated risks that are more likely to pay off.

In contrast, taking risks from a place of discomfort or chaos often leads to impulsive decisions, unnecessary failures, and wasted effort. By embracing comfort, you create a space where risks are approached deliberately and strategically, ensuring that each risk is a stepping stone toward sustained success, rather than a potential setback.

Why Comfort Enhances Risk-Taking:

- Calculated Decisions: Comfort provides the clarity and confidence needed to take risks that are well thought out and aligned with your long-term goals.
- Minimizes Reckless Behavior: When you operate from a place of comfort, you avoid impulsive risks driven by fear or pressure, focusing instead on those that offer real growth opportunities.
- Maximizes Success: Strategic risks taken from a place of comfort are more likely to result in success, as they're approached with clear judgment and purpose.

Comfort as the Foundation of Sustained Success

Embracing comfort isn't about avoiding challenges or staying stagnant—it's about creating the conditions for long-term growth and success. Comfort provides the stability, confidence, and clarity needed to make smart decisions, take strategic risks, and push your boundaries in a sustainable way. Rather than rejecting comfort in favor of constant discomfort, recognize the power it holds in helping you achieve your goals over the long term.

By using your comfort zone as a base for expansion, you can continuously grow without losing control, burning out, or feeling overwhelmed. Comfort, when understood and used wisely, is not the enemy of growth—it's the path to mastery, confidence, and lasting success.

Expanding Horizons Strategically

CHAPTER NINETEEN

Pushing Boundaries on Your Own Terms

The world that often glorifies aggressive leaps into the unknown, pushing boundaries is frequently seen as a radical, all-or-nothing endeavor. However, true, sustainable growth happens when you push boundaries on your own terms—with intention, strategy, and control. You don't need to chase discomfort or act recklessly to achieve success. Instead, you can expand your horizons by deliberately challenging yourself while still leveraging your strengths and maintaining control over your path.

Pushing boundaries on your own terms means expanding your comfort zone in ways that align with your goals, values, and pace, allowing you to grow without losing control or feeling overwhelmed.

1. Define What Growth Means to You

The first step to pushing boundaries on your own terms is to clearly define what growth means for you personally. Growth isn't a one-size-fits-all concept. For some, it might mean taking on new leadership responsibilities; for others, it might mean learning a new skill or improving an existing one. The key is to identify the areas where you want to push your boundaries in a way that is meaningful and relevant to your journey.

Instead of being influenced by societal expectations or external pressures, you must stay aligned with your own goals and vision for success. This helps you take control of your growth process and ensures that you're expanding in ways that matter to you, not just reacting to external noise.

How to Define Growth on Your Terms:

- Reflect on Your Goals: Identify what success and growth mean to you—both personally and professionally. What areas do you want to improve or expand?
- Ignore External Pressures: Resist the urge to compare your journey with others. Focus on growth that aligns with your values, strengths, and long-term objectives.
- Set Clear Intentions: Define specific areas where you want to push your boundaries, ensuring that each step forward has a clear purpose behind it.

2. Take Calculated Risks

Pushing boundaries doesn't mean taking reckless risks. When you push boundaries on your own terms, you do so with calculated risks that are aligned with your strengths and areas of expertise. Calculated risks are challenges that stretch you without completely overwhelming you, allowing you to grow without sacrificing stability or control.

By understanding your strengths and weaknesses, you can identify opportunities that are both challenging and achievable. These calculated risks lead to meaningful growth because they're backed by strategy, preparation, and a clear understanding of your limits.

How to Take Calculated Risks:

- Assess Your Strengths: Before stepping outside your comfort zone, evaluate your strengths and how they can be applied to new challenges.
- Weigh the Benefits: Ask yourself if the potential reward is worth the risk. Is this an opportunity that aligns with your goals? Will it help you grow in meaningful ways?
- Prepare and Plan: Minimize uncertainty by preparing for the risk. Build a plan for how you'll approach the challenge, what resources you'll need, and how you'll handle potential obstacles.

3. Expand Gradually and Strategically

Instead of diving headfirst into unknown territory, pushing boundaries on your terms means gradual, strategic expansion. You don't need to jump into discomfort to grow. By pushing your boundaries incrementally, you can expand your comfort zone in a way that is manageable and sustainable.

Each time you push the boundaries of your comfort zone, you're adding new skills, knowledge, or experiences to your existing base of expertise. This gradual expansion ensures that you're not overwhelmed by drastic changes and that each step forward builds on the last. Over time, what once felt like a stretch becomes a new part of your comfort zone, allowing you to continue growing confidently.

How to Expand Gradually:

- Break Challenges into Steps: Rather than tackling big challenges all at once, break them into smaller, more achievable steps that allow you to expand your comfort zone gradually.
- Focus on One Area at a Time: Avoid spreading yourself too thin by trying to push boundaries in multiple areas simultaneously. Focus on one area of growth at a time, ensuring that you're giving it your full attention and effort.
- Track Your Progress: After each step, reflect on your progress and celebrate small wins. This reinforces your sense of accomplishment and motivates you to keep pushing forward.

4. Stay in Control of Your Growth

Pushing boundaries on your own terms is about maintaining control over your growth process. You're not expanding for the sake of it—you're doing it with intention. This control allows you to decide when to push harder and when to step back and regroup. By staying in control, you ensure that your growth is aligned with your strengths, interests, and personal goals, rather than reacting impulsively to external pressures.

This approach also allows you to avoid burnout. When you're in control of how and when you expand, you're able to pace yourself, taking time to reflect and recharge when necessary. This ensures that your growth is sustainable and that you're not overextending yourself.

How to Stay in Control:

- Set Boundaries: Know when to say no to opportunities that don't align with your goals or that feel overwhelming. Pushing boundaries doesn't mean saying yes to everything.
- Pace Yourself: Avoid the temptation to push too hard, too fast. Take time to rest, recharge, and reflect on your progress before moving on to the next challenge.
- Adjust as Needed: Be flexible and willing to adjust your approach if things aren't going as planned. Staying in control means being adaptable and making decisions that serve your long-term success.

5. Use Your Comfort Zone as a Base

Your comfort zone is not a place to avoid or escape; it's a strategic base from which you can safely push boundaries. When you operate from your comfort zone, you have the stability, confidence, and clarity needed to take on new challenges without feeling overwhelmed.

Instead of abandoning your comfort zone entirely, you can expand it gradually, allowing you to grow while maintaining the confidence that comes from working within your strengths. This approach to pushing boundaries ensures that each new challenge feels manageable and that you're never out of your depth. Over time, your comfort zone will naturally expand to include more skills, experiences, and opportunities for success.

How to Use Your Comfort Zone as a Base:

- Leverage Strengths: Use the strengths and skills you've mastered in your comfort zone as a foundation for exploring new opportunities. When you push boundaries, do so from a place of competence and control.
- Recharge When Needed: After pushing boundaries, return to your comfort zone to reflect, regroup, and recharge before taking on the next challenge.
- Expand Strategically: Each time you push your boundaries, incorporate what you've learned into your comfort zone. This creates a continuous cycle of growth and mastery.

6. Prioritize Personal Fulfillment

Pushing boundaries on your own terms isn't just about professional success—it's also about finding personal fulfillment. Growth is most meaningful when it aligns with your passions, interests, and values. When you expand in ways that resonate with who you are, the journey becomes not just about achieving external success but also about enriching your life in ways that bring you satisfaction and joy.

Rather than chasing external markers of success, focus on growth that feels authentic to you. When you're pushing boundaries that align with your personal goals and values, the challenges you take on become opportunities for personal development, self-discovery, and long-term fulfillment.

How to Prioritize Fulfillment:

- Align Growth with Values: Choose challenges that reflect your values and passions, ensuring that your growth journey feels authentic and meaningful.
- Pursue Joy, Not Just Success: Push boundaries in areas that bring you joy or personal satisfaction, even if they don't directly lead to professional advancement.
- Reflect on Your Why: Regularly ask yourself why you're pushing your boundaries. Is it to achieve something meaningful to you, or are you reacting to external pressures?

The Power of Pushing Boundaries on Your Own Terms

Pushing boundaries doesn't have to mean stepping into chaos or constantly seeking discomfort. By doing it on your own terms, you ensure that your growth is purposeful, strategic, and aligned with your long-term goals. Whether you're expanding your professional skill set, pursuing personal passions, or exploring new opportunities, the key is to remain in control of how and when you push your boundaries.

When you expand gradually, take calculated risks, and use your comfort zone as a base, you can achieve sustained growth without feeling overwhelmed or lost. The journey becomes one of continuous mastery, confidence, and personal fulfillment, allowing you to push boundaries not because you have to, but because you choose to.

CHAPTER TWENTY

When and How to Step Out for Growth, Without Panic

Stepping outside your comfort zone is essential for growth, but it doesn't have to be a leap into chaos or fear. The key to effective growth is knowing when and how to step out of your comfort zone in a way that feels strategic, purposeful, and manageable—without triggering panic or overwhelming yourself. Growth is most sustainable when you approach it with intention and control, rather than anxiety and haste.

Here's how you can step out for growth in a way that fosters confidence and success, rather than panic and uncertainty.

1. Recognize the Right Time to Step Out

Timing is everything when it comes to stepping out of your comfort zone for growth. Not every moment is the right one, and not every opportunity is worth the risk. To avoid panic and ensure success, it's important to recognize when stepping out is truly beneficial.

The right time to step out is when you feel a natural pull toward growth, whether it's because you've outgrown your current environment, you're seeking new challenges, or you want to develop new skills. You don't need to force yourself into discomfort. Instead, look for moments when your skills, curiosity, or ambitions push you toward something new, but not overwhelmingly so.

How to Recognize the Right Time:

- Boredom or Stagnation: When you feel like you're no longer challenged, or your routine has become too predictable, it's a signal that you may need to step out to continue growing.
- Opportunities Aligning with Goals: If a new opportunity arises that aligns with your long-term goals or personal growth, it could be the right time to push your boundaries.
- A Feeling of Readiness: Pay attention to your internal cues—when you feel excited or motivated by the prospect of new challenges, rather than fearful or overwhelmed, it's a sign that you're ready.

2. Start Small: Take Gradual Steps

One of the most effective ways to step out for growth without triggering panic is by starting small. Growth doesn't have to come from a giant leap into the unknown—it can come from gradual, manageable steps that allow you to expand your comfort zone bit by bit. This approach ensures that you stay in control of your progress while reducing the risk of feeling overwhelmed.

Instead of throwing yourself into a completely unfamiliar or daunting situation, break the challenge down into smaller tasks. Each small step pushes your boundaries just enough to foster growth, but not so much that it triggers panic.

How to Take Small, Manageable Steps:

- Break Challenges into Pieces: If you're stepping into a new role or project, focus on mastering one aspect at a time rather than trying to do everything at once.
- Set Mini Goals: Create smaller, incremental goals within the larger challenge. This makes the process feel more achievable and reduces anxiety.
- Celebrate Small Wins: Acknowledge and celebrate each step forward, even if it seems minor. This builds momentum and confidence for larger challenges.

3. Prepare and Plan for Growth

One of the most common causes of panic when stepping out of your comfort zone is the feeling of being unprepared. To avoid this, make sure you prepare and plan before taking the leap. Preparation gives you the confidence and tools you need to succeed in new, unfamiliar situations. It also reduces the fear that comes from the unknown because you've taken steps to anticipate and address potential challenges.

When you prepare for growth, you approach it from a place of strength rather than fear. Whether it's acquiring new skills, seeking mentorship, or gathering resources, preparation helps you feel more in control of the process, making it less likely that you'll panic.

How to Prepare for Growth:

- Do Your Research: Before stepping into new challenges, research what you'll need to succeed. This might involve learning new skills, understanding potential obstacles, or seeking advice from others who've done it before.
- Create a Roadmap: Map out a step-by-step plan for how you'll approach the challenge. Breaking it into smaller steps helps you see the path ahead more clearly.
- Gather Resources: Whether it's skills, information, or support, make sure you have the resources you need to handle the challenge before stepping into it.

4. Stay Grounded in Your Comfort Zone

Stepping out of your comfort zone doesn't mean abandoning it entirely. In fact, you can step out for growth while staying grounded in the strengths and skills you've already mastered. Your comfort zone provides a stable foundation that allows you to face new challenges with confidence rather than panic.

By keeping one foot in your comfort zone, you maintain a sense of control and familiarity while gradually expanding into new areas. This approach helps you stretch your limits without feeling like you're diving into the deep end unprepared. Your comfort zone serves as your anchor, allowing you to explore new opportunities while knowing you have a place of stability to return to.

How to Stay Grounded While Stepping Out:

- Leverage Your Strengths: When taking on new challenges, lean on the skills and expertise you already have. This gives you a solid foundation from which to tackle unfamiliar situations.
- Return to Your Comfort Zone: After taking on a challenge, return to your comfort zone to reflect, regroup, and recharge. This helps prevent burnout and keeps you grounded.
- Expand Gradually: Instead of taking drastic leaps, push the boundaries of your comfort zone incrementally. Each time you step out, integrate what you've learned into your comfort zone, making it larger and more robust.

5. Manage Fear and Self-Doubt

Fear and self-doubt are natural responses when stepping into the unknown, but they don't have to lead to panic. Managing your mindset is key to stepping out of your comfort zone for growth in a way that feels empowering rather than overwhelming. By recognizing fear and doubt for what they are—temporary emotions rather than obstacles—you can approach new challenges with confidence.

It's important to remind yourself that fear and self-doubt are part of the growth process. The goal is not to eliminate them but to navigate them effectively. With practice, you'll learn to trust yourself in new situations and build resilience against fear-based reactions.

How to Manage Fear and Self-Doubt:

- Acknowledge Fear: Instead of trying to suppress fear, acknowledge it. Recognize that it's a natural part of the growth process and that it doesn't define your ability to succeed.
- Focus on the Learning Opportunity: Shift your mindset from fear of failure to the excitement of learning something new. Each challenge is an opportunity to grow and improve.
- Remind Yourself of Past Successes: When self-doubt creeps in, remind yourself of the challenges you've overcome in the past. Use those experiences as proof that you're capable of handling new ones.

6. Seek Support When Needed

Stepping out for growth doesn't have to be a solo journey. Having a support system in place can make the process more manageable and less intimidating. Whether it's a mentor, friend, or colleague, seeking support helps you feel more grounded and reassured as you step into new challenges.

Support provides not only encouragement but also practical guidance for navigating unfamiliar territory. A mentor who has gone through similar experiences can offer valuable insights, while a friend or colleague can provide emotional support and accountability.

How to Seek Support:

- Find a Mentor: Seek out a mentor who can guide you through new challenges, offering advice, feedback, and reassurance based on their own experience.
- Share Your Goals: Let others know about your growth goals and ask for their support. This could mean checking in regularly to keep you accountable or offering encouragement when you face challenges.
- Join a Community: If you're stepping into a completely new field or skill, consider joining a community or group of people who are also navigating similar challenges. This shared experience can make the process feel less isolating.

7. Pace Yourself and Know When to Step Back

Sometimes, growth requires knowing when to step back as well as when to push forward. If you start feeling overwhelmed or panicked, it's okay to slow down or return to your comfort zone temporarily. Pacing yourself is crucial to sustainable growth—it allows you to push your boundaries without burning out or losing your motivation.

Stepping back doesn't mean you're giving up; it's about regrouping and giving yourself the space to reflect and recharge. Once you've regained your confidence and energy, you can continue moving forward with a clearer mindset and renewed focus.

How to Pace Yourself:

- Recognize Overwhelm: Pay attention to signs of overwhelm that indicate you may be pushing too hard or too fast. If you notice feelings of anxiety, stress, or burnout, it's a sign that you may need to step back for a moment.

- Take Breaks When Needed: It's okay to pause and take a break from pushing your boundaries. Give yourself time to reflect, recharge, and regain clarity before moving forward again.
- Set Realistic Timelines: Don't rush the process. Set achievable timelines for your growth, allowing room for rest and reflection along the way.

8. Celebrate Progress and Reflect on Growth

Growth doesn't happen overnight, and it's important to celebrate your progress along the way. Each step you take outside your comfort zone is a win, no matter how small. By acknowledging your achievements, you reinforce your confidence and motivation to keep pushing forward.

Reflection is also key to understanding what worked, what didn't, and how you can improve in the future. By regularly reflecting on your progress, you can identify patterns, strengths, and areas for further development, ensuring that each step outside your comfort zone leads to meaningful growth.

How to Celebrate Progress and Reflect:

- Celebrate Small Wins: Acknowledge and celebrate each milestone, whether it's mastering a new skill or simply overcoming a fear. This boosts your morale and reinforces your efforts.
- Reflect Regularly: Set aside time to reflect on your growth journey. What did you learn? How did you

handle challenges? What can you do differently next time?

- Adjust Your Approach: Use reflection to make adjustments to your growth strategy. If something isn't working, tweak your approach to ensure you're pushing boundaries in a way that feels productive, not overwhelming.

Stepping Out for Growth, Without Panic

Stepping outside your comfort zone doesn't have to mean diving into panic or chaos. By approaching growth with intentionality, preparation, and gradual steps, you can expand your capabilities without losing control or confidence. Knowing when to push your boundaries and how to stay grounded in your strengths allows you to grow strategically, ensuring that each step forward feels both manageable and empowering.

With the right mindset, support, and pacing, stepping out of your comfort zone becomes a rewarding experience rather than a source of fear. Growth, after all, is not about rushing into discomfort but about expanding your potential on your own terms—without panic, and with lasting results.

Chapter 10: Reclaiming Comfort as Power

CHAPTER TWENTY-ONE

Why Comfort is the Key to Long-Term Success

In a world that often celebrates constant hustle and stepping into discomfort, comfort is often misunderstood as a barrier to growth. However, true, sustainable success isn't about living in a state of perpetual discomfort; it's about building a strong foundation within your comfort zone and expanding it strategically. When comfort is embraced and leveraged correctly, it becomes the key to achieving long-term success, creating a base of mastery, confidence, and resilience that supports continuous growth.

Comfort is not the enemy of success. In fact, it's the secret ingredient that allows you to operate with clarity, build long-lasting skills, and maintain a sense of balance and control, all of which are crucial for achieving and sustaining success over time.

1. Mastery is Built-in Comfort

One of the greatest advantages of operating from a place of comfort is that it enables you to develop mastery. Mastery doesn't come from constantly jumping into new and unfamiliar challenges; it comes from practicing and refining your skills until they become second nature. Your comfort zone is where you develop this expertise, allowing you to perfect your craft and achieve excellence.

Rather than seeking discomfort for the sake of growth, comfort allows you to focus on deepening your knowledge and enhancing your abilities within a familiar space. As you become more skilled and confident in your area of expertise, you position yourself for long-term success because you've built a solid foundation of mastery that you can rely on, no matter what challenges come your way.

Why Mastery Matters for Long-Term Success:

- Consistency of Performance: When you've mastered your craft, you deliver consistent results, building a reputation for reliability and excellence.
- Deep Expertise: Mastery gives you a competitive edge, as fewer people take the time to fully develop their skills before moving on to the next challenge.
- Confidence in Action: Operating from a place of mastery means you have the confidence to handle even unexpected challenges, ensuring that you can maintain success over time.

2. Comfort Provides Clarity and Focus

Comfort allows you to operate with clarity and focus, both of which are essential for long-term success. When you're in a state of comfort, your mind isn't overwhelmed by stress, fear, or uncertainty. Instead, you're able to make thoughtful, strategic decisions that align with your goals.

This clarity helps you stay focused on the bigger picture, rather than getting distracted by short-term challenges or external pressures. By operating within your comfort zone, you can prioritize effectively, make better decisions, and execute your plans with precision. This kind of focus and intentionality is what sets successful people apart—they don't waste time or energy on unnecessary distractions, but instead stay committed to their long-term vision.

How Comfort Creates Clarity:

- Mental Space for Strategic Thinking: Comfort gives you the mental clarity to think strategically and plan for the long term.
- Focused Execution: Without the constant noise of uncertainty, you can focus on executing your plans with greater precision and effectiveness.
- Purposeful Decision-Making: Operating from comfort allows you to make decisions based on logic and strategy, rather than reacting impulsively to discomfort or stress.

3. Comfort Builds Confidence Over Time

Confidence is a crucial element of long-term success, and it doesn't come from pushing yourself into panic or discomfort—it comes from mastering what you do best. When you operate from your comfort zone, you develop a deep sense of confidence in your abilities, because you're building on skills you've already honed.

This confidence grows as you continue to refine and perfect your abilities within your comfort zone. Over time, the more you succeed within this space, the more trust you build in yourself. This confidence enables you to take on new challenges without fear because you know you can rely on your strengths.

Confidence isn't about faking it or pretending to be comfortable in uncomfortable situations; it's about being grounded in what you know and trusting your ability to expand that knowledge as needed.

Why Confidence is Key to Long-Term Success:

- Reduces Fear of Failure: When you're confident in your abilities, you're less likely to be paralyzed by fear of failure, allowing you to take calculated risks.
- Enables Strategic Growth: Confidence allows you to push boundaries in a measured way, ensuring that each new challenge feels manageable and rewarding.
- Inspires Trust: People are more likely to trust and follow leaders who exude confidence, making it easier to build influence and maintain success over time.

4. Comfort Creates a Space for Innovation

Innovation doesn't always happen in moments of discomfort. In fact, some of the greatest breakthroughs come from deep thinking within a space of comfort, where your mind is free from stress and survival mode. When you're comfortable, you have the mental bandwidth to explore new ideas, experiment, and find creative solutions without the distraction of fear or panic.

By using your comfort zone as a base, you can explore innovative approaches to challenges without feeling overwhelmed. This safe space allows for risk-taking and experimentation in a controlled way, giving you the opportunity to innovate while still maintaining stability.

How Comfort Supports Innovation:

- Freedom to Experiment: Comfort gives you the stability to explore new ideas and approaches without the fear of immediate failure.
- Mental Clarity for Problem-Solving: Operating from a calm, stable place allows you to think creatively and solve problems more effectively.
- Sustained Innovation: Innovation is more sustainable when you can balance experimentation with a strong foundation of expertise and confidence.

5. Comfort Allows for Sustainable Growth

Pushing yourself into constant discomfort can lead to burnout. On the other hand, operating from a place of comfort allows for sustainable growth. You're not depleting your mental, emotional, or physical energy by constantly living on the edge. Instead, you're growing at a steady pace, expanding your comfort zone in a way that ensures long-term success without the risk of exhaustion.

Comfort also provides the opportunity to rest and recharge when needed, which is crucial for maintaining the energy and focus required for sustained success. By embracing comfort, you avoid the trap of constant hustle and instead create a balanced approach to growth that allows you to thrive over the long term.

Why Sustainable Growth is Important:

- Prevents Burnout: Comfort gives you the opportunity to rest and recharge, ensuring that you don't exhaust yourself in the pursuit of success.
- Enables Long-Term Success: Sustainable growth is about playing the long game—expanding at a pace that allows you to build on your success without sacrificing your well-being.
- Maintains Motivation: Comfort ensures that you remain motivated over time, as you're not constantly overwhelmed by stress or uncertainty.

6. Comfort Enhances Resilience

While discomfort is often associated with building resilience, comfort can also foster resilience by giving you the space to reflect on challenges, learn from them, and apply those lessons in a controlled environment. When you face challenges from a place of comfort, you're better equipped to process setbacks and bounce back with greater strength.

Resilience isn't just about enduring hardship—it's about learning how to navigate challenges in a way that doesn't overwhelm you. By staying grounded in your comfort zone, you can face difficulties without losing control, allowing you to recover quickly and continue growing.

How Comfort Builds Resilience:

- Controlled Environment for Learning: Comfort allows you to process challenges in a controlled environment, where you can learn and adapt without feeling overwhelmed.
- Space for Reflection: Reflecting on setbacks from a place of comfort helps you gain perspective and use challenges as opportunities for growth.
- Foundation for Recovery: When challenges arise, your comfort zone provides a stable foundation that allows you to bounce back more effectively.

Comfort as a Catalyst for Long-Term Success

Comfort isn't a barrier to success—it's a powerful tool that, when used correctly, can be the key to achieving and sustaining long-term success. By embracing comfort, you create the space for mastery, clarity, confidence, and innovation, all of which contribute to sustained growth.

Rather than constantly seeking discomfort, recognize the value of operating from a place of strength and stability. Use your comfort zone as a foundation from which you can expand, innovate, and grow—strategically and sustainably. In doing so, you'll find that comfort isn't just a resting place; it's the catalyst for long-term success, resilience, and fulfillment.

CHAPTER TWENTY-TWO

Reframing the Comfort Zone for Peak Performance

The comfort zone has long been mischaracterized as a place of complacency and stagnation—a space where nothing significant happens and no growth occurs. However, when you reframe the comfort zone, you begin to see it for what it truly can be: a launchpad for peak performance. Rather than abandoning your comfort zone, you can use it strategically to optimize your skills, maintain focus, and push your boundaries in a controlled, productive way.

By reframing the comfort zone, you create a new narrative—one that embraces comfort as a powerful tool for achieving peak performance, rather than a limitation. Here's how you can reframe and leverage your comfort zone to unlock your full potential.

1. The Comfort Zone as a Space for Mastery

Peak performance is built on mastery, and mastery requires repetition, practice, and refinement—none of which can be achieved in a constant state of discomfort. Your comfort zone is where you develop deep expertise and hone your skills to a level where they become second nature. This is the space where you can perfect your craft, allowing you to perform at your absolute best when it matters most.

Rather than seeing the comfort zone as a place to avoid, it's crucial to view it as the foundation of mastery. Mastery doesn't happen in chaos—it happens in stability. By operating from a space of comfort, you can refine your abilities, build confidence, and deliver consistent, high-quality results.

How Mastery in the Comfort Zone Enhances Peak Performance:

- Repetition Leads to Precision: The more you practice within your comfort zone, the more precise and effective you become, leading to higher levels of performance.
- Automatic Responses: Mastery turns complex actions into automatic responses, allowing you to focus on execution without second-guessing.
- Foundation for Complex Challenges: With a strong foundation of mastery, you can take on more complex challenges without being overwhelmed, elevating your performance when faced with new situations.

2. Comfort Enhances Focus and Clarity

One of the most underrated benefits of the comfort zone is that it creates the mental clarity and focus needed for peak performance. When you're in a space where you feel confident and competent, your mind isn't clouded by stress, fear, or anxiety. Instead, you're able to direct all of your energy toward focused execution—the kind that drives peak performance.

Operating in comfort doesn't mean staying idle—it means being in a state of flow, where you can engage deeply with your work and achieve high levels of concentration and productivity. This focus enables you to accomplish more in less time, with greater efficiency and accuracy.

How Comfort Supports Focus for Peak Performance:

- Distraction-Free Execution: In your comfort zone, you can focus solely on your work without the distractions of uncertainty or self-doubt.
- Flow State: Comfort allows you to enter a flow state, where you're fully immersed in your tasks and can perform at your highest level.
- Improved Decision-Making: With clarity comes better decision-making, allowing you to solve problems and tackle challenges more effectively.

3. Leveraging Comfort for Strategic Expansion

The idea that you must constantly step far outside your comfort zone to grow is a misconception. Instead, you can leverage your comfort zone to strategically expand into new areas, pushing your boundaries in a way that feels manageable and controlled. This method of gradual expansion ensures that you stay in command of your growth process, allowing you to build on your strengths while minimizing the risk of burnout or panic.

By expanding the edges of your comfort zone, you can incorporate new skills, knowledge, and experiences into your repertoire without feeling overwhelmed. Each time you push the boundaries of your comfort zone, you're growing without sacrificing performance, ensuring that you continue to operate at your peak.

How to Strategically Expand Your Comfort Zone for Growth:

- Set Incremental Challenges: Rather than taking huge leaps, break down growth into smaller, achievable steps that stretch your abilities while still feeling manageable.
- Use Your Strengths: Leverage your existing strengths as a foundation for taking on new challenges, ensuring that each step forward builds on what you already know.
- Reflect and Adjust: After each step, reflect on your progress, integrate what you've learned, and adjust your approach to ensure continuous growth without overwhelm.

4. The Comfort Zone as a Recovery Space

Peak performance requires periods of recovery and reflection. Operating at a high level for long stretches without breaks can lead to burnout, diminished performance, and decreased motivation. The comfort zone provides a much-needed space to recover, recharge, and regain focus before taking on the next challenge.

When you reframe the comfort zone as a strategic tool for recovery, you allow yourself to perform consistently at your highest level. This balance between challenge and recovery is what enables long-term success. The comfort zone isn't a place of laziness—it's where you refuel so that you can come back stronger and more focused than before.

Why Recovery in the Comfort Zone is Crucial for Peak Performance:

- Prevents Burnout: Regular recovery within your comfort zone ensures that you avoid burnout and stay energized for new challenges.
- Reflective Space: Comfort allows you to reflect on your progress and learn from your experiences, improving performance over time.
- Maintains Motivation: By balancing intense effort with periods of comfort, you sustain your motivation and enthusiasm for growth.

5. Comfort Builds Resilience for Long-Term Success

Success doesn't come from constant discomfort—it comes from building resilience over time, and the comfort zone plays a crucial role in this process. By operating from a place of comfort, you create a stable environment where you can develop emotional resilience, which is essential for handling setbacks, challenges, and uncertainty without losing momentum.

Your comfort zone provides the emotional security needed to bounce back from failures and adapt to new situations. Resilience isn't just about enduring hardship; it's about navigating challenges with confidence and control. When you use your comfort zone to build resilience, you're better equipped to handle the ups and downs of life and work without sacrificing performance.

How Comfort Builds Resilience for Peak Performance:

- Emotional Stability: Comfort creates a foundation of emotional stability, allowing you to recover from setbacks quickly and keep moving forward.
- Strengthened Coping Mechanisms: When challenges arise, your comfort zone gives you the mental and emotional space to process them without feeling overwhelmed.
- Long-Term Endurance: Resilience ensures that you can maintain peak performance over time, handling both successes and failures with grace and perseverance.

6. Reframe Discomfort as Strategic Growth, Not Constant Necessity

While discomfort is often presented as a requirement for growth, it doesn't need to be a constant state. Instead of jumping headfirst into chaos, discomfort should be strategic and intentional. When you reframe the comfort zone for peak performance, you recognize that stepping into discomfort should happen only when it serves a clear purpose and when you've prepared yourself adequately.

Strategic discomfort—such as taking on a new challenge or learning a new skill—is more impactful when you do it from a place of confidence and readiness. This way, you're pushing yourself toward growth in a way that elevates your performance rather than undermining it.

How to Reframe Discomfort for Strategic Growth:

- Prepare Before You Step Out: Before stepping into discomfort, ensure that you've built a strong foundation within your comfort zone so that you can handle the challenge with confidence.
- Pace Yourself: Don't feel pressured to constantly operate outside your comfort zone. Pace your growth, allowing time for recovery and reflection.
- Evaluate the Purpose: Only step into discomfort when it serves a clear purpose for your long-term goals, ensuring that the challenge aligns with your vision for peak performance.

Reframing the Comfort Zone for Peak Performance

The comfort zone is not a place to escape or avoid—it's a space to embrace and optimize for peak performance. By reframing the comfort zone as a foundation for mastery, focus, and strategic growth, you unlock your ability to perform at your highest level without sacrificing well-being or control.

Peak performance comes from balancing comfort with growth, using your comfort zone as a space to refine your skills, recover when needed, and push your boundaries in a controlled and intentional way. When you reframe the comfort zone, you stop seeing it as a limitation and start using it as a powerful tool for achieving long-term success and excellence.

Conclusion: The Uncommon Perspective on Success

CHAPTER TWENTY-THREE

Embracing Comfort as a Vantage Point

The idea that comfort leads to stagnation has long been popular, but what if comfort is actually a vantage point? Rather than being a place of complacency, your comfort zone can be the strategic high ground from which you gain perspective, control, and insight—giving you the ability to navigate challenges more effectively and pursue growth on your terms. Embracing comfort as a vantage point allows you to operate from a place of strength and mastery, making thoughtful, confident decisions that propel you forward.

In this context, comfort doesn't mean playing it safe or avoiding risk. Instead, it's about using your established strengths as a launchpad for growth, allowing you to observe new opportunities with clarity and act with purpose. From this vantage point, you can see the bigger picture and make strategic moves that lead to long-term success.

1. Comfort as the Base for Clear Decision-Making

When you operate from a place of comfort, you gain the

mental clarity needed to make sound decisions. Without the distractions of fear or uncertainty, you can assess challenges and opportunities from a place of confidence. This clarity allows you to see the path ahead more clearly, giving you the perspective necessary to identify the best course of action.

By staying grounded in your comfort zone, you give yourself the advantage of seeing situations from a calm and stable perspective. This vantage point lets you make decisions based on long-term goals rather than reacting impulsively to external pressures. It's not about avoiding challenges, but about ensuring that you're approaching them from a place of control and purpose.

How Comfort Enhances Decision-Making:

- Reduced Noise: Without the mental clutter of stress or uncertainty, you can focus on the key factors that matter most when making decisions.
- Big-Picture Thinking: Operating from comfort gives you the headspace to think about the long-term impact of your choices, rather than being caught up in short-term challenges.
- Informed Choices: With a clear mind, you can evaluate your options more thoroughly, ensuring that each decision aligns with your overall goals.

2. Comfort as a Position of Strength

When you embrace comfort as a vantage point, you're operating from a position of strength. Your comfort zone represents the mastery, skills, and experiences you've built over time—things you do well and can rely on. From this position, you can confidently expand into new areas without feeling overwhelmed or losing control.

By recognizing the power of your comfort zone, you acknowledge that you have a strong foundation from which to push boundaries. This foundation allows you to stretch your limits while maintaining the confidence that comes from your existing expertise. You're not leaping into the unknown; you're taking calculated risks from a place of preparedness and strength.

How Comfort Provides Strength:

- Mastery as a Foundation: Your comfort zone is built on mastery, allowing you to perform at your best in familiar situations and tackle new challenges with confidence.
- Controlled Growth: From a position of strength, you can push boundaries strategically, ensuring that each step forward is well-supported by your skills and experience.
- Confidence in Execution: Comfort gives you the confidence to execute tasks effectively and efficiently, knowing that you have the skills to succeed.

3. Comfort as a Launchpad for Exploration

Rather than seeing the comfort zone as a limitation, reframe it as a launchpad for exploration. From this vantage point, you can safely step out and explore new opportunities while staying connected to your base of strength. The comfort zone serves as your grounding—the place where you can retreat to reflect, recharge, and refine your approach.

By using your comfort zone as a launchpad, you ensure that you're not taking reckless risks but rather strategic leaps. This allows you to test new skills, explore different avenues, and take on challenges without feeling like you're completely stepping into the unknown. Your comfort zone gives you the advantage of knowing you can always return to a place of security and control when needed.

How to Use Comfort as a Launchpad:

- Step Out, but Stay Connected: Push your boundaries, but always maintain a connection to your comfort zone, using it as a place of stability when navigating new challenges.
- Return for Reflection: After exploring new opportunities, return to your comfort zone to reflect on your experiences, evaluate your progress, and plan your next steps.
- Gradual Expansion: Treat your comfort zone as a launchpad for gradual expansion, where each new experience builds on your existing strengths and confidence.

4. Comfort as a Source of Perspective

Operating from comfort gives you the perspective needed to see opportunities and challenges with a clear, strategic mind. When you're not operating in survival mode, you have the ability to step back and view situations from a wider angle, seeing connections, patterns, and potential solutions that might otherwise be missed in a state of stress or discomfort.

This bird's-eye view of your situation allows you to make better decisions, identify growth areas, and approach challenges with a more measured, thoughtful strategy. Comfort gives you the time and space to understand the landscape before you act, ensuring that your moves are informed by careful observation rather than reaction.

How Comfort Offers Perspective:

- Big-Picture Awareness: Comfort allows you to see the full scope of a situation, helping you make more informed decisions based on long-term goals.
- Strategic Insight: From a place of comfort, you can identify opportunities for growth that align with your strengths, making your approach to challenges more strategic.
- Measured Risk-Taking: When you have the advantage of perspective, you can take calculated risks that are well thought out, increasing the likelihood of success.

5. Comfort as a Recharge Point for Resilience

Your comfort zone isn't just a place for stability—it's also a recharge point that fuels your resilience. Stepping out of your comfort zone for growth is important, but doing so constantly without breaks can lead to burnout. By embracing comfort as a vantage point, you create a space where you can recover and regroup after facing challenges, allowing you to maintain high levels of performance over the long term.

Comfort provides the mental and emotional energy needed to face new challenges with renewed strength. By returning to your comfort zone when needed, you can reflect on your experiences, learn from setbacks, and recharge before taking on the next challenge. This cycle of growth, recovery, and reflection is what enables long-term success and resilience.

How Comfort Fuels Resilience:

- Rest and Recharge: Use your comfort zone as a place to rest and recharge after periods of growth or challenge, ensuring that you avoid burnout.
- Reflective Learning: After facing new challenges, return to comfort to reflect on what you've learned and how you can apply those lessons moving forward.
- Resilience for Future Growth: By using your comfort zone to recover, you build the resilience needed to take on bigger challenges without losing momentum or motivation.

6. Using Comfort to Expand Your Influence

Operating from a place of comfort doesn't mean staying small—it means expanding your influence from a stable, confident base. As you grow more skilled and comfortable in your abilities, you can use your comfort zone as a platform to expand your influence, whether that's in your career, leadership, or personal development.

By being in a place where you are fully in control of your strengths, you're better positioned to lead, inspire, and influence others. You can take on bigger challenges and responsibilities without feeling overwhelmed because you're operating from a place of confidence and mastery.

Over time, this leads to greater influence and impact, as others recognize your ability to navigate challenges with calm and control.

How Comfort Expands Influence:

- Confidence in Leadership: Operating from comfort gives you the confidence to take on leadership roles and influence others through your actions and decisions.
- Leading by Example: When others see you operating from a place of comfort and strength, they're more likely to trust your judgment and follow your lead.
- Expanded Reach: As your comfort zone expands, so does your influence. You can take on bigger projects, roles, or responsibilities while maintaining the confidence that comes from your strengths.

Comfort as Your Strategic Vantage Point

Comfort doesn't limit your growth; it enhances it by providing a vantage point from which you can see clearly, act confidently, and navigate challenges with precision. When you embrace comfort as your base of strength, you gain the advantage of perspective, control, and resilience—essential elements for long-term success.

By using your comfort zone as a strategic vantage point, you can push boundaries without losing your footing, make informed decisions that align with your goals, and maintain the resilience needed to thrive in the face of challenges. Comfort is not a place to avoid—it's your launchpad for strategic growth, allowing you to expand your horizons with purpose and clarity.

CHAPTER TWENTY-FOUR

Living Powerfully Within Your Mastery Zone

True lasting success comes from mastering what you do best, not from endlessly chasing the unknown. Your mastery zone is the space where you operate with skill, confidence, and control—the place where you're most capable of delivering powerful results consistently. By embracing and living powerfully within this zone, you unlock a level of excellence that leads to greater impact, influence, and fulfillment.

Living within your mastery zone doesn't mean playing it safe. It means leveraging the skills and expertise you've developed over time to perform at your highest potential, creating a strong foundation from which you can strategically grow and expand.

1. Mastery as a Source of Confidence

The power of living within your mastery zone comes from the confidence it gives you. Mastery is built through repetition, experience, and deliberate practice—when you've mastered a skill, you don't need to second-guess yourself. You know what you're doing, and you can approach tasks and challenges with a deep sense of self-assurance.

This confidence translates into powerful execution. When you live within your mastery zone, you perform tasks with precision and ease, knowing that you have the capability to deliver high-quality results. This consistent excellence doesn't just lead to better outcomes; it also boosts your confidence in taking on more complex challenges as you expand your zone of mastery.

How Mastery Builds Confidence:

- **Repetition Breeds Expertise:** Mastery is achieved through consistent practice, allowing you to become deeply skilled in your craft.
- **Automatic Responses:** As you master your abilities, complex tasks become automatic, freeing up mental energy to focus on strategy and innovation.
- **Confidence in Execution:** With mastery, you approach every task with confidence, knowing that you can execute it effectively and efficiently.

2. Mastery as a Path to Consistent Excellence

One of the key benefits of living within your mastery zone is the ability to deliver consistent excellence. When you've honed your skills to a level of mastery, you can rely on them to produce outstanding results time and again. This consistency is what sets apart those who succeed in the short term from those who achieve long-term success.

By living within your mastery zone, you develop a reliable process for achieving success. Whether you're solving problems, leading teams, or creating products, the expertise you've built ensures that your performance remains consistently high. This not only enhances your reputation but also builds trust with those who rely on you—whether they're clients, colleagues, or collaborators.

How Mastery Leads to Consistent Excellence:

- **Reliability in Results:** Mastery allows you to deliver predictable, high-quality outcomes, making you a go-to person in your field.
- **Refinement of Process:** With each repetition, you refine your approach, making your process more efficient and effective.
- **Excellence Becomes the Standard:** As you live within your mastery zone, excellence becomes your baseline, ensuring that your performance is always at its peak.

3. Mastery as a Launchpad for Strategic Growth

Living powerfully within your mastery zone doesn't mean standing still—it means using your mastery as a launchpad for strategic growth. When you operate from a place of mastery, you have the confidence and clarity to push boundaries in a controlled and deliberate way. Instead of diving into unknown challenges blindly, you expand your skills gradually, ensuring that each new area you explore builds on your existing expertise.

This approach to growth ensures that you're constantly evolving without losing the control and stability that comes from operating within your mastery zone. You're not abandoning what you know; you're strategically building on it, expanding your comfort zone and skill set while maintaining a high level of performance.

How Mastery Fuels Growth:

- **Expanding Comfort Zones:** Mastery allows you to push your boundaries in a measured way, growing without sacrificing confidence or control.
- **Layering New Skills:** As you master one area, you can layer new skills on top of it, creating a deeper, more versatile skill set.
- **Strategic Risk-Taking:** With a foundation of mastery, you can take calculated risks that align with your long-term goals, ensuring that each new challenge contributes to growth.

4. Mastery as a Tool for Influence and Leadership

Living within your mastery zone gives you the power to influence and lead others. Mastery breeds confidence, and confidence is magnetic. People are naturally drawn to those who are highly skilled and able to deliver results consistently. When you operate within your mastery zone, you set an example for others, leading by your actions and the results you produce.

As a leader, your mastery allows you to make decisions with clarity and authority. Others trust your judgment because they see your expertise in action. This positions you as a leader who not only inspires but also delivers, building a reputation for strong, results-driven leadership. Your mastery also enables you to mentor and guide others, helping them develop their own skills and reach their potential.

How Mastery Enhances Leadership:

- **Trust and Respect:** People trust and respect those who consistently deliver high-quality results, making you a natural leader.
- **Influence Through Example:** Your mastery sets a powerful example for others, showing them the value of dedication and expertise.
- **Mentorship Opportunities:** As a master in your field, you have the ability to mentor others, helping them grow and succeed under your guidance.

5. Mastery as a Catalyst for Innovation

Mastery doesn't stifle creativity—it frees you to innovate. Once you've mastered the foundational skills of your craft, you're free to explore new ways to solve problems, create solutions, and push the boundaries of your field. Operating within your mastery zone gives you the confidence to experiment and innovate because you're grounded in your expertise.

When you're not bogged down by uncertainty or the basics, you can focus on elevating your work. This leads to breakthroughs and innovative ideas because you have the mental space to think creatively and experiment with new approaches. Mastery provides the structure you need to take creative risks with confidence, knowing that even your risks are calculated.

How Mastery Fuels Innovation:

- **Freedom to Experiment:** With the basics mastered, you have more freedom to explore creative solutions and experiment with new ideas.
- **Confidence to Take Risks:** Mastery gives you the confidence to take creative risks, knowing that you have a strong foundation to fall back on.
- **Enhanced Problem-Solving:** When you're operating from a place of mastery, problem-solving becomes more intuitive, allowing for innovative approaches to challenges.

6. Mastery as a Source of Fulfillment

Living powerfully within your mastery zone isn't just about achieving external success—it's also about finding deep personal fulfillment. Mastery brings a sense of accomplishment and pride in your work, knowing that you're operating at the highest level of your abilities. This leads to a greater sense of purpose and satisfaction, as you're fully engaged in your work and confident in your ability to make a meaningful impact.

Mastery also allows you to enjoy the process of your work. When you're deeply skilled at what you do, the act of doing it becomes rewarding in itself. This sense of fulfillment goes beyond external recognition or success—it's the internal satisfaction that comes from knowing you've put in the time, effort, and dedication to achieve mastery.

How Mastery Leads to Fulfillment:

- **Sense of Accomplishment:** Mastery brings a deep sense of pride and accomplishment in your work, knowing that you're performing at your best.
- **Purposeful Work:** When you're operating within your mastery zone, you're fully engaged in your work, leading to a greater sense of purpose and satisfaction.
- **Enjoyment of the Process:** Mastery allows you to enjoy the process of your work, as each task is a demonstration of your skills and expertise.

Living Powerfully Within Your Mastery Zone

Living powerfully within your mastery zone is about recognizing the strength and potential that comes from operating at your highest level. By embracing mastery, you unlock the confidence, consistency, and influence needed to achieve lasting success. Your mastery zone is where you perform at your peak, delivering excellence with ease and pushing the boundaries of your abilities in a controlled, deliberate way.

Rather than constantly seeking the unknown, use your mastery zone as a launchpad for growth. By building on your strengths and expanding strategically, you create a pathway to success that's not only sustainable but deeply fulfilling. Mastery isn't about playing it safe—it's about living powerfully within your strengths and using them to create a lasting impact on your field, your career, and your life.

End Note

Own Your Zone, Define Your Success

As we come to the end of Inside The Comfort Zone, I hope this book has given you a new perspective on growth, mastery, and success. You don't need to abandon what you know or throw yourself into discomfort to grow. Real, sustainable success comes from owning your strengths, mastering your craft, and expanding your comfort zone on your own terms.

The world often glorifies struggle, chaos, and the idea that success is only for those who constantly push themselves into uncertainty. But time and again, the most successful individuals—whether in business, art, sports, or leadership—have shown us that mastery within the known leads to excellence. They have honed their expertise, deepened their skills, and built their influence from a place of strength—not struggle.

Your Comfort Zone is Your Power

Instead of chasing discomfort for the sake of it, use your comfort zone as a base of confidence and a launchpad for innovation. Expand it intentionally, step beyond it when necessary, but never abandon it. Growth should not feel like survival—it should feel like an evolution of what you already do best.

- Master what you know.
- Push boundaries on your own terms.
- Stay in control of your growth.

- Define success in a way that aligns with your strengths.

You Are in Charge of Your Story

Success is not a one-size-fits-all formula. You get to decide how you grow, how you challenge yourself, and how you build a life of impact and fulfillment. Whether you're an entrepreneur, a student, a professional, or a creative, remember this: you don't need to fit into someone else's definition of success. Your zone, your strengths, your path—own them.

Thank you for being part of this journey. I hope this book becomes a guide, a reminder, and an inspiration for you to live powerfully within your mastery zone and redefine success on your terms.

Here's to mastering your comfort zone and building a future where success feels as natural as it should.

Stay confident. Stay powerful. Stay in your zone.

To Your Success,
Ashish Gupta

www.ingramcontent.com/pod-product-compliance
Lightning Source LLC
La Vergne TN
LVHW091317150826
845673LV00006B/1680